The Long Ride Home

The Long Ride Home

A Life in the Minnesota Music Scene

Mick Sterling

CROTALUS

THE LONG RIDE HOME
A life in the Minnesota Music Scene

Published by:
CROTALUS PUBLISHING
3500 Vicksburg Lane North #302
Plymouth, Minnesota 55447-1333
www.crotaluspublishing.com

ISBN 0-9741860-5-8

Cover and book design by Michelle L.N. Cook
Cover photo © Dāv Kaufman
Author photo/front flap by Marc Norberg

When possible, photo credits are given to the photographer.
Sorry, but Mick just can't remember them all.

Library of Congress data on record.

Crotalus and the Rattlesnake Colophon
are trademarks of Crotalus Publishing.

First Printing, July 2005

Printed in Canada

Contents

My Immediate Family
My beautiful wife, Kristi, my amazing children, Mikaela and Tucker, my strong Italian mother, Neva, my four brilliant sisters, Debbie, Toni, Peggy, and Jessica, my father, Robert Jensen, all my nieces and nephews, Judy and Dave Knutson, Tony Knutson, Kerrie Hailey, Kerissa and Preston Hailey

Friends and mentors from my early days
Erik Elias, Peter Bratsch, Peter Guertin, Annie Miners, Shannon Herman, and teachers who changed my life: Miss Christensen, Mr. Stahn, Mrs. Dorenfeld, Mrs. Goodwin, Gary and Carole Fisher, and Mr. Hermerding

The core players in the history of the Stud Brothers and other projects
Mark Moran, Tim Moran, Jeff Fideler, Layne Bender, Bernie Edstrom, Charles Fletcher, Billy Franze, Mara Jacob, Bobby Vandell, Pat Mackin, Emanuel Kiriakou, Rob Arthur, Donnie LaMarca, Steve Pikal, Bob Hallgrimson, Joe DeRasmi, Brian Simonds, Mark Lickteig, Kevin Bowe, Andy Dee, John Haga, Dik Shopteau, Marv Gohman, Rick Vanbergen, Rich Dreyer,

Mark and Julie Boatman, Joe Rumbolo, Kevin Broccard, John Orlando, Brad Murphy, Annie Clifford, Ken Abdo and the Abdo Family, The Abdomen, James Klein, Jackie Kelly, Jimmy Hefferan, Miki Nord, Ted Koenecke, Mike Kelly, Grant Scherer, Dan LaFond, Dale Ann Murphy, Susan Leckey, Neil Willenson, the children of Camp Heartland, Sara Sanders, the children of Camp Odayin, Micha McFarlane, Mark Kanter, Mark McGowan, Mike and Kirsten Beach, Sue McLean, Billy Larson, Jadin Bragg, Rex Buxton, Steve DeVries at Showcore, Steve at Blackhawk , Ted Ewing at Skyway Tent Rental, Heidi Sammon, Jim and Cindy from The Narrows, all the volunteer leaders from Heart & Soul, all of the artists who have performed at Heart & Soul, Tommy Azzone, Barb Lyke, Jonny Lang, Brian Leighton, Renee Austin, Brad and Nicole Thompson, Maurice Jolly, Lori Barbero, Tom Asp, Marc Norberg, Electric Fetus, Tom from *NiteTimes Magazine,* Bayfront Blues Festival, Noiseland Industries, Copy Cats, Craig Scofield, Bahram Akradi and everyone at Lifetime Fitness, UPS for keeping my family secure, all the people who take time out of their lives to come and see me sing, and all the clubowners and festival organizers who hire me.

n the summer of 2003, the publisher of a Twin Cities music publication, *NiteTimes Magazine,* asked me to write a monthly column. The initial intent was for the column to concern itself with local bands, updates on who was coming in concert, etc. As I read the magazine, it was obvious that other contributing writers already covered those particular subject matters. I thought it might be a good idea to dig a little deeper. I wanted to share some stories and my opinions on the local music scene, as well as people and events who have molded me in to the performer, the husband, the father, and the man I am today. Writing these columns has given me an enormous amount of pleasure. In the process, I've discovered that what I'd written had struck a nerve with many of the musicians and music fans in the Twin Cities. I want to take this opportunity to publicly thank Tom from *NiteTimes Magazine* in the Twin Cities for giving me the opportunity to open up this new chapter in my life. I've been performing professionally for just over twenty years. I don't consider myself an expert in the music business by any stretch of the imagination. However, longevity has its advantages, so I guess through sheer persistence, I've learned a few things. I'm presenting observations on things that I have some level of sure footing. I openly admit right now that I will not touch on a huge portion of popular music in the Twin Cities. I am not learned in the history of any style of music like a record reviewer or musical historian is. I'm confident that I've missed some that I should have reached. My apologies go out to those I missed. Getting all the stories of the Twin Cities music scene will take someone with more knowledge than I have. It also requires many more pages than my publisher is willing to commit to this project. I recommend that if you want to find out more about the Twin Cities scene in the past and present, there's plenty of material out there to validate the rich history of music there.

I think the biggest objective for me in writing this book is to get across the human side of this business. It can be humbling one minute and rewarding the next. As potentially glamorous and financially lucrative as it can be, it's easy to see why people would find it fascinating. However, the kind of mass adulation and success that people see happening to the top-line artists happens so rarely.

It makes me wonder why people still attempt it. The odds are so overwhelming against that kind of success. Thankfully, there will always be a kid out there with a beat-up old guitar and a yearning to learn his first chords. There will always be the kid singing to records in his or her room trying to hit those notes that their idols reach so effortlessly. With music so easy to download, kids can hear a wider and broader musical spectrum in a far quicker and cheaper way than I was able to. Hopefully, they will dig a bit deeper than what is on the radio and find out why their heroes today sound that way.

The musicians and other participants in the business in this book were all driven early to achieve their version of "The Dream." Some reached their goals, some fell far short, some settled for their position, some gave it up and wised up and found a far more stable way to make a living. Like the profession of acting, the majority of musicians have had to find other ways to make a living, either on the way up, during the ride, or on the way down. What may separate being in the music business from other ventures is the unmistakable need to be seen, to create, to inspire, and to reach people. It must be those things, because it sure isn't for the ultimate payoff. It's a dream worth pursuing though; I still go for it, just a bit differently these days.

Basically, I'm a meat and potatoes kind of singer. Sometimes it ain't pretty, but I have my moments. But unlike some singers, I know where my bread is buttered. I couldn't do what I do without the great caliber of musicians supporting what I am trying to express. Leading the group of musicians that make up Mick Sterling and the Stud Brothers has been the focal point of my professional life for more than fifteen years. There have been many members who have come and gone in the band, and some who have stayed for the long haul. In the past five years, I've been a song writing and live performing partner with Kevin Bowe and his band, the Okemah Prophets, which we now call The Rolling Blunder Revue. I received invaluable advice from Twin Cities based Jazz trumpeter and former member of the band, Bernie Edstrom, about asserting myself to be a band leader. I've received great advice from many of my band members throughout the years. Cowriting with former members Emanuel Kirakou and Rob Arthur, and currently with Donnie LaMarca, Billy Franze, and Mark Lickteig has been very rewarding. The Stud Brother Horn Section, who have been with me since the beginning, Bob Hallgrimson and Steve Pikal have provided each version of the horn section the stability and the power that separates them from the rest. I want to thank all of the musicians who have graciously decided to stick with me.

I admit it; I am a glass half full kind of person. I'm able to be that kind of person because all my life I have been surrounded by the love and support of my family. My mother, Neva, is a strong Italian woman who raised my four sisters, Debbie, Toni, Peggy, and eventually, my little sister Jessica. My mother is a brave and proud woman who taught me many things. She was there for me during all the tough times in my childhood. She drove me to rehearsals, listened to me sing songs, went to my plays, and basically loved me. I love her dearly. My older sisters, Deb, Toni, and Peggy, were fantastic to me. I was the one they all looked out for. Deb had to do a lot of the hard work in the family when Mom was off working as a waitress bringing in the money to keep us living in our house. Throughout all the struggles (most of which I am sure they shielded me from), they encouraged and embraced me. I got my turn to play that role for my little sister, Jessica, in her early years.

All of these things molded me into the ninth grader that a girl named Kristi Knutson first saw at Plymouth Junior High School for an audition of an improvisational troupe. She was stunning. She blew my mind. We became friends but she intimidated me for many reasons. Life as a junior high student can be very humiliating and confusing. Thankfully, we all grow out of that eventually. As luck would have it, in my early twenties, Kristi walked into my life again, this time inside Bunkers Music Bar and Grill. We saw each other and it was all over. It has been more than twenty years since that fateful day at Bunkers and nearly thirty years since Plymouth Junior High. I married Kristi Knutson. She blessed me with two incredible, funny, intelligent, and tenderhearted kids, Mikaela and Tucker. Strong women and a father who did the best he could have guided me all my life. That's a big reason why I'm a glass half full kind of a guy.

An extension of my performing and recording career has been producing charitable events featuring live music from local and national artists. I've experienced some fantastic highs and some heartbreaking lows doing these events. Creating the concert series Heart & Soul took my life in a new direction. Through the volunteerism of hundreds of committed and inspired souls, we were able to help generate exposure and send a lot of money to Camp Heartland, a place for kids living with HIV/AIDS. Heart & Soul was—and is—a huge part of my life. I wish to thank everyone at Camp Heartland for having the faith in me to contribute to the lives of the children who attend your camp. Although our paths have separated a bit the past couple of years, good work was done in our time together that helped kids. That's all you can ask I suppose.

I love this business. I know how lucky I am to be a survivor of it. I know what it's like to sit in the crowd and have a band move you. I know what it's like to long to do what that person you are watching is doing. I know how hard it is to find the right combination of players to create what you want to express. It takes hard work and a lot of good luck and timing to take it to the next level.

There are a million stories floating around about how tough and unfair this business is. Some are based on some facts; most have probably been embellished through the years. Reality tells me that this business is what you make of it. What it gets down to is that the musicians who have taken to the stage in various nightclubs and theaters the past fifty years know they've been lucky to do it. Despite all the hardships that befell them and will surely befall the people presently performing as well as future artists, we will still drive to the club and do our thing. We get to do something that the vast majority of people will never experience. It's still about the song. Finding the right chord structure or finding just the right lyric to tell your story can give you a feeling like no other. People applaud when you finish your job. Not many jobs will do that. No matter how far along any musician is, or no matter what form their career is taking, one basic principle will always remain consistent. A gig is still a gig and if you have one, you're damn lucky.

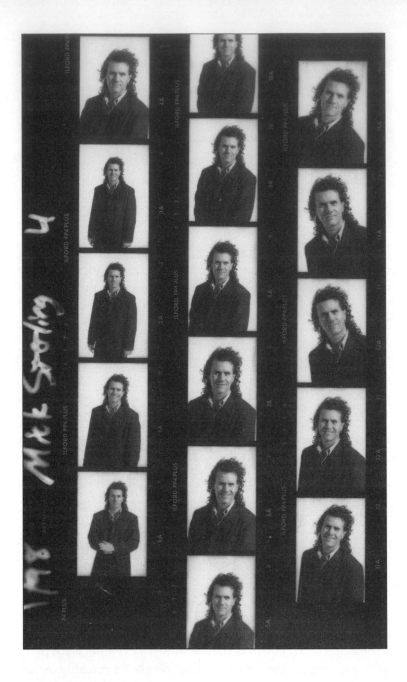

I know what you're thinking. Hey, it was the early '90s. My hair was enthusastic at that photo shoot. I used to have a fine head of hair. I cut it a few years later after I saw a guy my age with the same kind of hair. Photo shoots are never easy. Not my strong suit.

Beginnings

I grew up with three older sisters. Before I was five years old, I lived in many places in Minnesota and California. When we returned to Minnesota, we shared a house for six months or so with one of my mom's friends. She had four kids and a husband and a couple of huge poodles. We had my older sisters, my mom, and sometimes my dad (that's another story). Somehow, we all survived in that madhouse until Mom found a house nearby for us to move into. When we did, I shared a room with my sister Debbie. Debbie was kind of like a second mom to all of us at the time. Mom had to work nights as a waitress, so Deb would make sure we did what were supposed to do. I had a little record player from Montgomery Wards that sat on the floor, near our bedroom door. Many mornings, I would wake up before Debbie, turn the record player on, and sing softly along with the music. It always woke her up but she didn't seem to mind too much, or at least I don't remember her minding. I suppose subconsciously, it was payback for her talking in her sleep all night. It kept me awake, trying to figure out what she was saying. It didn't feel like payback when I was six, I just loved music and I knew I could sing a little bit. I was a pretty cute kid though back then. I probably could have gotten away with a lot more if I had wanted to.

I wish the next portion of this story had more meat to it. I wish the content that follows would give the people who see me sing in the Twin Cities a clear insight as to why I sound the way I sound. I wish my influences were tied to the legendary figures of blues, soul, and rock. They're not. I was a six year old in a suburb of Minneapolis called Crystal. My Montgomery Ward record player was not spinning the Beatles, the Stones, Muddy Waters, James Brown, Otis Redding, The Doors, Wayne Cochran, Etta James, Hendrix, and other influential figures at that time. I woke my sister up each morning to the band that introduced me to rock and roll. The band that made me want to be in a band. The band that guided me in my first venture of singing in public. I even had a guitar with the band members' faces on it. My introduction to rock and roll was by the Monkees. My first 45 was "I'm a Believer." The first TV show that really made an impression on me was *The Monkees*. Wait, I take that back, there were two. The other one was *Get Smart* with the beautiful Barbara Feldon. She made this six-year-old boy feel kinda funny in my strange place sometimes. Despite my six-year-old lust for Barbara Feldon, The Monkees were it for me. I remember getting in a big argument with a neighbor about who was better, The Monkees or The Beatles. It was so obvious to me at the time that The Monkees were the best so it wasn't even worth getting mad about. The Monkees were on TV every week. They were played all the time on the Twin Cities pop station, KDWB. They wore cool red shirts with the buttons in a different part of the shirt. They had cool boots and that big round belt buckle. They were zany and did crazy things. A couple of times during the show they would break into song. These were songs I could sing along with. I memorized them back and forth and burned that old Montgomery Ward record player out. After everyone was awake in the house, I would sing those songs at full voice. I knew all the words, and I made sure all my sisters knew it.

I received a Monkees guitar for my birthday one year. God, I loved that guitar. It was a guitar you couldn't play. It didn't have a recording of a Monkees song if you pressed a button. It was just a plastic guitar with four cheap strings.

The guitar had pictures of Mickey, Davy, Peter, and Mike and the Monkees logo. I'd play that guitar in my room along with the songs and sing along. I rocked as hard as a six-year-old could to songs like "Star Collector," "Valerie," "Pleasant Valley Sunday," "I'm Not Your Stepping Stone," and many others. I sang to the Monkees so often that I got a little cocky. I decided to take my show on the road.

My version of the road was Yunkers Park. It was down the hill, just past the house with the really mean and crazy black lab that was always chained up, foaming at the mouth. This wasn't my first live performance. But it was my first attempt to sing for kids my age. My first live performance was at a bar in Golden Valley called The Point. My mom and dad worked there. Sometimes on Saturday afternoons, one or both of them would take me down to the bar with them to hang out with their friends. The bartender's name was Irv. He was a really tall, silver-haired guy that always put cherries in my glass of Coke. I liked Irv. At the bar, they had a huge jukebox that was directly across from the bar. Sometime during the afternoon, the same request would come from Irv and my parents. It was time for me to sing. I guess I had to pay for those cherry Cokes somehow.

The song was "King of the Road" by Roger Miller. I think it's safe to say that there was not a five-year-old in the world that owned that song like I did in Golden Valley in the '60s. I would stand up on that jukebox with Roger Miller music playing, and I worked the few people sitting at the bar as I sang along at the top of my lungs. I shudder to think what I must have sounded like. Now that I'm a parent, I can assume it must have seemed very charming. I do remember, even back then, really liking the positive response I would get from the people in the bar. To be fair, those people at the bar weren't going to boo a five year old singing, they weren't made of stone. Whatever their motivation was to applaud, I liked it.

My success at The Point and my constant rocking with my Monkees guitar led me to the picnic bench at Yunkers Park. It was where I had the brilliant idea to sing all the Monkees songs I knew to the kids at the park during the summer. Now, you have to remember, this is 1967. Kids played outside all the time. No computers, no video games, no nothing. You were either outside or you were stuck in the house doing chores. The park was always packed. I was convinced they needed entertainment, and I was just the kid to do it.

The picnic bench was my stage. I stood on that bench and I did my thing. I can't remember how many times I performed on that park bench. I don't even remember how the kids liked it. The only thing I remember was that I made the Yunkers Park Newsletter one week. The short story was about my performances, with a quote from my sister Toni. When she was asked what she thought about her little brother, she said she just felt "embarrassed." Despite her feelings, or however many times I'm sure I drove my sisters crazy with my singing, they let me do it. I'm forever grateful for that. They watched out for me.

Those were the days when I began to love music. As someone who's sung for thirty-eight years—professionally for twenty-four years—I try and resurrect those feelings I had when I just loved music. It thrilled me. It excited me. Hearing new music was always exciting. If I could sing along with it, all the better. It's as if music played a nurturing role in my life. Outside of the actual record in your hand, the power of what music provided me was palpable. It defined me. As a six-year-old, I didn't know what that meant. The only thing I knew was that I had to have it in my life.

Eventually, singing along with a record just doesn't do it anymore. The next step is finding other people to play with. For me, that happened one day when I was in eighth grade.

I was an extremely short and very shy kid. I had just survived a very tough first year in junior high: new school, new kids from other schools, all the awkward things that early teenagers deal with. I felt like I dealt with all of them twenty-four hours a day. As I entered eighth grade, the second year of junior high, I could tell things were going to be a bit easier. It was during this time that I met the person who played the largest role in what I'm doing today. It happened in the smelly locker room of Plymouth Junior High School. As any boy will tell you, the smell of a boys' locker room is one that never leaves you: the combination of sweaty jocks (they made us wear them, but most of us didn't quite need them yet, I know I didn't), the old gym clothes jammed in those tiny lockers they gave you, and the overwhelming stench of the collective insecurity of showing our naked bodies to other kids. Some kids got hair before some others, I'll just leave it at that.

As I walked in to the locker room one morning, I heard someone shout, "I'll give you $12 for that shirt!" I looked up and saw this kid with long hair and glasses running toward me. The shirt I was wearing that day was a red "Elton John's Greatest Hits" t-shirt. Now you have to remember that $12 back in 1974 to a thirteen-year-old was a lot of money. I could have bought two records with that money and still had money left to go to McDonalds. Thankfully for me, realizing I didn't have another shirt to replace the shirt this kid offered to buy from me, and also realizing I didn't want to walk around shirtless exposing my barely hairy and acne-filled teenage chest to the other kids at school, I turned down his offer. He probably didn't have the money on him anyway, come to think of it. Nobody I knew had $12 on them back then. This kid, his name is Peter Guertin, left the locker room without my shirt, but he didn't leave my thoughts. During our time in the locker room, we started talking about how we both loved Elton John. As I was talking to Peter, I remembered where I had seen him before. He played at the talent show in Plymouth. He dressed up like Elton, played piano, and fronted his own band with a drummer, bass, and guitar player. He performed this in the big stage in the gym. He was phenomenal.

Peter played the piano like Elton. He sang like Elton. He dressed like Elton and did all his moves. He drove all the junior high kids crazy with what he was doing. I'm sure if I watched a film of that performance, the band probably wasn't that good and the sound quality was undoubtedly terrible in that gym. None of that mattered to me when I was in the crowd. This was someone my age, playing live rock and roll, and he was spectacular. People were screaming. He was singing and playing at the same time. It was everything I dreamt it would be. But this time it wasn't a dream. It was real and happening in my school.

Peter and I saw each other again a couple of days later. We started talking about maybe someday going over to his house. The deal was, he would play, I would sing. From the first note that Peter played on his piano in his basement and from the first line of the Elton song I sang that day, my life, for better or for worse, forever changed.

From that moment on, Peter and I hung out a lot. We would hang out at our friend Annie's house and play songs. Annie played piano for me when I auditioned for an improvisational group in ninth grade called Soup Group. The song I auditioned with was "Burn Down the Mission," an Elton John song, of course. This audition is also the first time I met the girl who would eventually become my wife. She sang the Band-Aid theme song, "I am stuck on Band-Aids, cause Band-Aids stuck on me!" Elton's song was better, but who cares? Kristi was driving me and every other boy in the audition crazy.

Soup Group was my first experience with singing to a crowd with a real sound system and microphone. Our teacher was Ert Hermerding, who I'm sure was the only drama-football coach in the history of American schools. Ert was a huge inspiration to me. He insisted that this improv group have a real sound system to perform on as we traveled with our show to different schools in the district. He lobbied the school to pay for a real sound system, and he got one.

It was my first time singing with a real microphone. It felt good. I knew I sang differently from the other kids in school. My confidence was starting to grow. I knew that acting was really not my strong suit, so I knew singing was the thing that would get me where I eventually wanted to go.

Music played such a huge role in my life as a teenager. I was blessed to have people like Peter and Annie who shared their talent with me. Friends would come over to Annie's house and sit there kind of stunned as we sat and sang songs for them. Just like I did back at Yunkers Park, our friends didn't really ask for it, we just assumed they would want to hear it. Although we didn't acknowledge it back then, I'm convinced deep down that we knew what we were doing was special. It played a huge role in our eventual professional careers and our outlook on life.

In that same summer, my dad invited Peter and me to come to a house party his friend was throwing. When I heard who was throwing the party, I knew it was going to be one of those parties that would probably last a couple of days. My dad had a lot of friends in the bar business. One thing that will never change is that people in the hospitality industry know how to party and don't grow weary of partying. It seems strange to me now that my dad would invite a couple of fourteen year olds to an adult party, but I didn't question it at the time. We'd go anywhere for free food.

As we walked to the house around three in the afternoon, the attendees of this party were already feeling extremely happy. Lots of hugging, lots of yelling, and lots of only God knows what was going on. I've been around that stuff before, so it didn't really matter to me. What was becoming evident to Peter and me was that there really wasn't much to do for a couple of fourteen-year-old kids. We were growing bored with it and decided to go home. Just as we were leaving, the host of the party and my dad came up to us and said there was a piano in the garage. They asked us if we would want to pull it out and do some songs. We checked it out.

The piano was an old beat-up stand-up piano with gold lamé hanging from the back of it. It must have come from some bar that the party's host had worked at one time in his life. It had a bunch of crap sitting on it and was filled with dust and wood shavings. We cleaned off the piano and pulled it out of the garage. We pushed that piano out to a cement slab attached to the garage facing the backyard. It was horribly out of tune and some of the keys were pretty beat up. It wasn't quite a ragtime sound, but the piano had seen better days before we got to it. As the party continued on, Peter played and I sang.

As was our custom back then, we did primarily Elton songs, with a couple of Beatles songs thrown in. No microphone for the piano or my voice. Nobody really acknowledged us as we played. But they weren't telling us to shut up either, so we just kept playing. After about ninety minutes or so, we decided to take a break to get something to eat in the house. We were gone for about thirty minutes or so, eventually finding our way back to the piano. When we arrived, we found something sitting on the piano that shocked and puzzled us: a snifter glass full of dollar bills and quarters.

We looked around trying to figure out how this glass of bills got on the piano. Who put it there? Whose money is it? Should we just take it and run? We didn't know. I asked my dad about it. He just said the people at the party decided to tip us a bit for our songs. He said he didn't tell anybody to do it, but I'm sure he encouraged it. Anyway, as the snifter jar was continually being filled with dollar bills, we kept playing until we ran out of songs to play. My voice was shot. Peter's fingers were damn near bleeding because the keys were so coarse and jaded. We came, we saw, we conquered. Michael and Peter had left the building!

As we rode our bikes to my house, we didn't say much. As soon as we got to the driveway, we took out all the money and started counting. When we were done counting, it wound up being $34. Thirty-four dollars! We made money playing songs. Someone actually decided to give us money for doing what we do for free damn near every day. No agent fees, just the two of us. Seventeen dollars a piece. Our first paid gig. It was sweet.

Now I know that $17 doesn't seem like much, but for two teenagers in the mid '70s, $17 could buy a lot. That was almost three records we could get from our local record store, Down in the Valley. I could go golfing a couple of times at the par 3. It didn't really matter what I spent it on. What made it so special was that this money came from doing something we loved doing. It was all downhill—or uphill—from that moment on, depending on how I felt each day.

I loved this hat. Where it is now, who knows? I've lost a closet full of clothes and accessories in various clubs in the nation. This was taken at the Grandma's Marathon Tent Party in Duluth, Minnesota. Lots of exhausted runners and their crazed supporters. It's a good party.

When do we break and where the hell is my towel?

Chapter 2

When **7 was a high school student,** I went to the sophomore version of the Sadie Hawkins dance at Armstrong Senior High School in Plymouth, Minnesota. We called it Sno-Daze, for no particular reason. As the years have passed, my recollections of that dance have softened. I'm sure it wasn't as pathetic as it seemed, but the feelings were real.

I was extremely short in stature and very lonely most of that first year of high school. A lot of my friends from junior high made new friends once they got in high school. I spent a lot of time alone, looking pathetic and not hiding it very well to the other kids in school. I wore the same clothes for weeks at a time, watched a lot of TV, and listened to Elton John and Springsteen constantly. I loved music, but I hadn't played live music with a band for more than a year.

I hadn't seen a live band perform locally either. I knew it was something I wanted to do, I just had no idea how to make it happen. I perceived myself as a loser, (drama king, high school emotions taking over), my creativity was absorbed by my self-pity.

Somehow, a girl took pity on me and asked me to Sno-Daze. I was 25 percent of a double date that was going nowhere fast. I was intimidating myself all night, even while the girl I was with was valiantly trying to salvage the evening. The one saving grace was the live band performing that night.

This was 1977. From the time you woke up, rode on the bus back and forth to school, and sat in your room at night talking to your friend on the phone, you were surrounded by songs from The Eagles, Steve Miller, Elton John, Aerosmith, Led Zeppelin, Peter Frampton, Lynyrd Skynrd, Allman Brothers, Boston, Van Halen, Pink Floyd, and the Stones. My kids have asked me if I listened and liked these groups back then. My reply was, outside of Elton John, I never went out of my way to buy records by the popular artists of that time. As far as me liking these groups, there was no way to avoid these songs. As corny as this sounds, it was the soundtrack of our lives back then.

At this dance, the powers that be in the all-too-powerful student council, decided to give the people what they wanted. We wanted the songs we know, and we wanted to dance and, hopefully, make out either on the dance floor or later in a car or some other uncomfortable place. The name of that band was Some State . . . I think. It's a hazy, hazy mystery.

Through my fifteen-year-old eyes, playing this dance must have been a big deal to this band. Through their eyes, their emotions could have gone a thousand different ways. Just the fact that they were playing a high school dance may have driven them to finish off that bottle of Jim Beam with another bottle of Jim Beam. The eighteen-inch raised stage with golden tassels surrounding it could definitely not be confused with the stage at the Bottom Line in New York City.

I've been asked to perform at high school reunions. I want none of it. That is one of the lines I'll never cross. I enjoy playing too much to go down that road of humiliation. I was asked to play at my own high school reunion a while back. No thanks. If I was in a high school band playing a high school dance, fantastic. I couldn't imagine a bunch of forty- to fifty-year-olds playing for high school students, let alone a reunion of my age group. But for a fifteen-year-old kid who dreamed of playing in a band, playing at a high school dance seemed pretty glamorous to me. They played. Girls stared. People clapped. It was loud. What more would you want?

Three times that night, something happened that I couldn't quite understand. The band stopped. They left the stage and stood directly behind it talking to each other and other kids at the dance. They didn't look tired. We were all standing there with nothing to do. Why would they stop playing? Why would you want to stop playing if you were in a band? I looked for someone who resembled a manager to ask them why the band stopped playing. I was far too intimidated to go up to one of the band members and ask. They looked bored when they were on break. It looked like they needed something to do. Why didn't they just go back on stage and play until the dance was supposed to be over? That was my introduction to how bands, no matter how small or large, expect things. If they don't get it, they'll complain. They only played forty-five minutes each time they before took a break. Even at my tender age, I knew no other job lets you do that. Once you start playing live in clubs or private settings, you realize the beauty of the break. It works on so many levels for everyone involved. It's also the cause of a lot of tension between band members and club owners.

When I started playing in clubs in the '80s, most of the time you had to play four forty-five-minute sets with fifteen-minute breaks. I once played in a club in Granite City, Illinois, that required the band to play six sets, nine o'clock at night to three o'clock in the morning, six nights a week. That was brutal. There's not a band alive that is interesting enough to hear them

When do we break and where the hell is my towel?

play that many sets per night. At clubs like this, the chances are very good that the club owner will be sitting at the bar looking at his watch, timing the length of your breaks. I've often wondered if, when the club owner decided to own a club, they would have dreamed they would spend so much time angrily looking at their watch, trying to find a reason to hassle or dock the band's pay.

It's been my experience that the most successful clubs are run by owners who embrace the musicians and make them feel comfortable. The majority of the bands will reciprocate and go the extra mile for the club. Of course, there are exceptions. Some bands are, just by nature, annoying and abusive to any authority. The difficult bands don't seem to last long in club land. These club owners don't sweat if a band takes a few minutes longer on their break, but they also expect you to deliver when you play.

One element of the break is very simple. Band breaks give the audience members' ears some time to recover. The director of the sound you hear is the soundman. Even the best bands are slaves to the will and ears of whoever is mixing them. If the soundman is bad, it's a painful experience for the band and for the people in the club. When you're on stage and you can tell the volume is truly hurting people and irritating them, it's a helpless feeling. While it's a natural assumption to blame the band if it's loud, most of the time, there is more blame to go around. Most of the time, it's the soundman that is dictating what is happening in front of the stage.

It's an unusual relationship between the musician and the soundman. You'd think that because so much is riding on the soundman for a successful performance, the soundman would be king. Most of the time, it seems to be just the opposite. Many times soundmen are disrespected and not considered in the same league professionally. Many times, that sentiment from the musician is met with indifference, or hang dog acceptance from the sound tech. The good sound techs don't let anybody treat him disrespectfully. Coincidentally, if the soundman were great, the band wouldn't even think of mistreating them because a good soundman is so precious.

There are different types of loud when you see a band. That's why when you have a good soundman, you do damn near anything to keep him. When I first started playing clubs in the Twin Cities, I used to play at a place called Mr. Nibs. At this time, the club had the main room and the backroom. I was in a new band so I played the backroom. When I would get done with my set, I would go and see the main room band. The majority of the time I played at the club, the main room band was one of the funkiest, tightest bands I have ever seen to this day, the Doug Maynard Band. The band was filled with some superior players featuring Bobby Vandell on drums, John Della Salva on guitar, Ricky Peterson on Hammond organ and Jeff Boucher on guitar. The background vocals were handled by two of the sexiest women I had seen on stage, who just so happened to be able to channel Chaka Khan and Bonnie Raitt at anytime, the incomparable Margaret Cox and Melanie Rosales. Steve Raitt did the mix in the room.

This was the first time I had heard a soundman take control of a band and really stroke and stoke the room. He made everybody shine, especially the front man of the band, the legendary singer Doug Maynard. Doug was never demonstrative in his physical presence on stage. He rarely moved, but he didn't need to. He had the voice, this mysterious and deeply soulful voice, that amazed you. As a young man just starting to play in clubs, it was a mixture of intimidation and inspiration watching the Doug Maynard Band. The groove was so thick and deep and the sound coming from the stage was glorious to me.

Doug's vocals were unlike any I have ever heard. Many people would compare him to Joe Cocker. I always thought that was far too easy a comparison. His voice had far more versatility than Joe Cocker's voice in my opinion. As someone who was just beginning my club career, seeing Doug Maynard and the depth of the musical talent supporting him was pivotal. Some people have commented that Doug's voice and my voice have similar features. I consider that an extreme compliment.Doug was truly a gifted artist. He is missed in this town.

The longer I perform, the more I'm convinced that too many local musicians expect perks. They expect these perks even if they have to change into their stage clothes in the men's stall at the club. Tribute bands, hotel bands, cover bands, and even karaoke wannabes will let the little things dictate their performance. All of these musicians are aiming to reach, or they've convinced themselves they are at the level of deserving the holy grail of rock-and-roll perks: the plain and puffy white towel.

The puffy white towel is the benchmark for all local musicians. A towel must be nearby at all times. The guitar player needs a few. The drummer needs more because he sweats more than anybody. The keyboard player usually only needs one, unless he moves a lot. The bass player, if he plays his role right in the band, should only need a moist towelette or perhaps a double ply tissue. Bass players normally stand still and lay the groove down, and God bless them for that! In a perfect world, all lead singers should have a minimum of five towels per night to soak up all the sweat they'll generate. I'm sure I haven't gotten a record deal yet because of the lack of towels nearby when I perform.

Why do musicians covet the towel? Why can't we wipe our sweat on our shirt or our pants? Sometimes the sweat gets in your eyes, but do you need a huge towel for that? How about a handkerchief? It would be funny to see a bunch of handkerchiefs on the stage. If musicians had handkerchiefs instead of towels, it would have the same effect on them as Nigel Tufnel's battle with the small bread and cold cuts in Spinal Tap. There's no way we can work with handkerchiefs, it ain't rock and roll.

Like the majority of things having to do with popular music, the towel could be easily attributed to Elvis. I never saw Elvis in his Vegas phase in the '60s, but I do remember hearing something about scarves.

I remember that he would toss his sweaty scarves out to the screaming middle-aged women in the audience each night. Later I remember seeing him on his last recorded concert throwing those towels out again. Sadly, he threw them out as he incoherently mumbled through "Hound Dog." His bloated face looked pained, lost, and bored. Ever the professional, Elvis satisfied his audience by throwing out the scarves. Those who caught his scarves undoubtedly treasure them to this day. Why anybody wants a scarf in the first place though is still a mystery to me. Those scarves later morphed into puffy white towels for the rest of us. Elvis set the standard again for all rockers to follow.

The placement of the towel on stage is also very important. You can't just throw towels all over the stage willy-nilly. That confuses and angers musicians. There is a method that must be followed.

How you fold the towel is very important. You don't want to fold it too many times. If you do, it's too small. If you don't fold it enough, it's too big. You can't put all the towels behind one guy on stage and expect everyone to get their own. Walking the five to ten feet to get them is simply out of the question. Each towel must be placed where each member will be standing and stacked neatly on top of each other, or sitting comfortably close together. The gap between towels can't be too far, or one of the towels you use may belong to another member of the band. Once the towels are placed on stage that means the band is truly ready to play.

Once the performance starts, it's very important that you have a stockpile of additional towels on hand just in case. Outside of Elvis, I've never seen any musician throw their towel out to the crowd. They are too precious. If you're a real rock star, you'll have someone on hand to walk on stage while you're playing and replace your towel with a fresh one. Once the performance is done, it's normally the job of the band tech to collect all the towels, put them in a bag and clean them for the next performance.

I've seen performances held up for minutes because of the absence of towels. I've seen people scramble all over trying to find anything resembling towels so the band could perform. I've seen people who never move on stage, people who couldn't break a sweat if they were playing guitar in a sauna, withhold their performance until they received a towel. It's as if the towel has hypnotized us in to believing that our show will suck without them.

What's peculiar to me is that I never remember the artists who really needed towels, having towels. I saw James Brown at The Cabooze in Minneapolis in 1981. The room was a hot, packed, sweaty hothouse of funk and soul that night. James's band was as funky and tight as I dreamed it would be. James was of course sweating the instant he hit the microphone. He just kept sweating. No towel was necessary for the Godfather of Soul.

I saw Springsteen at the St. Paul Civic Center while he was promoting the "Darkness on the Edge of Town" record. The E Street Band was, without a doubt, the biggest and coolest collection of guys I'd ever seen. Springsteen of course left it all on the stage that night as he always does. The Boss didn't need a towel. He wiped his sweat on his shirt and rung it out dripping on the stage like a man.

The towel is not the most flamboyant rock-and-roll perk, but it's the most accessible for local bands. When you're playing in a club, you'll get the beer, the free drinks and sometimes the food. But you won't get the separate dressing room, catering, champagne, special fruit, etc. The one thing damn near every club can provide you is towels. We know it and we milk it for all it's worth.

It's the local musicians cotton touchstone to the big time. Long live the dream. When you're in a local band, you get to work sixty minutes three times a night and take two twenty-five-minute breaks. For that, people applaud you when you complete each task. When you're not playing, you get to speak to friends, and you meet new people who think what you do is fascinating, even if you're playing in a dump. When you're sweaty, someone provides you with a clean white towel for you to wipe your brow, chest, and forearms. Who else gets this kind of treatment? No one I can think of. For the record, I don't use towels, they embarrass me. But just the fact that the option of having a towel within reach is comforting in some green M & M-rock-and-roll way.

My first CD. I remember sitting at Metro Studios in Minneapolis alone in the studio, listening to it in its entirety. It was cool for me. It didn't set the world on fire, but it was fun to do. Our new audience seeing us at Bunkers loved bringing us home with them.

The world according to Mustang Sally and Brown Eyed Girl

"Mustang Sally" and "Brown Eyed Girl." The two songs that are the equivalent of the line in the sand for any musician playing in the clubs. They are the two songs that can direct the rest of the night for the majority of the musicians performing in clubs around the nation, and perhaps many clubs internationally. Musicians have to make their choice each night. This decision is not based in the immediate request, it's based on a decision they made long ago as to how they would pursue their musical dream. The audience member will only know if the band plays it or doesn't play it. For many club-goers, it will dictate how they feel about the band they are seeing depending on if they play one or both of those songs. Rest assured, if the band plays "Mustang Sally" or "Brown Eyed Girl," there was a struggle going on inside that musician far ahead of the request. Every genre of music has the songs that always get requested by club-goers. It may be a cover, or it may be your own song. What you do when you get the request is always a struggle.

I've never been able to figure out what it is about those songs that connects with people so strongly. The obvious answer would be the call back and sing-a-long opportunities. "Mustang Sally" has "Ride Sally Ride" and

"Brown Eyed Girl" has the always dependable "Sha La La." Those are easy to wrap your arms around and easy for anybody to remember and sing. But there are other songs out there with the same attributes. Why those two songs?

In order to get closer to an answer, let's acknowledge that a fact is a fact. "Mustang Sally" and "Brown Eyed Girl" are two amazing songs. There's a reason why those songs have lasted. They've stood the test of time and musical fads. It's hard to remember that when you're faced with playing either song every night. Most times, I'm sure musicians don't remember that. Any songwriter would be extremely happy getting the check in the mail for how many times those songs have been performed, recorded, heard on a TV and/or film soundtrack, background music for industrial use, etc. When Wilson Pickett sang "Mustang Sally" and Van Morrison sang "Brown Eyed Girl," they probably didn't realize how their lives changed. I'm sure they also didn't realize the effect it would have on club bands around the world. Every blues, soul, R & B, wedding, or corporate band out there definitely owes them a debt of gratitude. Most bands probably wish those songs never had been written because they're sick of playing them. I'm sure Van Morrison and Wilson Pickett probably wish they hadn't recorded the songs many nights for the same reason. Because just as local musicians get requests for the same songs, so do the legends. A song they recorded forty years ago is the only song their audience really wants to hear. When you see Wilson Pickett, he has to do "Mustang Sally." When you see Van Morrison, his audience wants him to do "Brown Eyed Girl." If they don't hear their favorite song, it will dictate how you feel about their performance, no matter how great every other performance was on the other songs they chose. It's the great equalizer for local and national acts. Same issues, larger stage.

Songs appearing in films have a powerful effect on the public. Soundtracks are a great vehicle for many artists to breathe new life into an old song. It might even help a song that may not have been a hit on their own record to become an eventual hit. It all depends on the placement of the song in the film. In the film *The Commitments,* the upstart, sloppy, and wonderfully cocky Irish band covered many great soul songs, including "Mustang Sally." The singer in that movie sang the hell out of those songs. That film also energized the song and made a deep impression for the people who saw the film. The film captured (perhaps unintentionally at the time) the brilliance of that song. It's a song that is a perfect fit for a nightclub setting. It's a song that even if you don't sing, you could fantasize about yourself singing that song. You can see yourself singing "All I wanna do is ride around Sally" and the crowd yelling back, "Ride Sally Ride." That film gave "Mustang Sally" another fifty years of life. Another example of the power of film and song is the Sam and Dave classic, "Soulman," that was featured in the film starring John Belushi and Dan Ackroyd, *The Blues Brothers.* I've always thought that film didn't get its due respect for what it accomplished. Blues purists have scoffed at the legitimacy of the Blues Brothers Band ever since their debut. While it is true that what they produced was musically borrowed from the greats, and it may have begun as the concept for a great comedy sketch, what it accomplished was monumental to acceptance of blues and soul in the late '70s through today.

A strong argument could be made that the Blues Brothers could be the blues equivalent for what Elvis Presley did for rock and roll. Many people consider Elvis' "That's Alright Mama" or Bill Haley's "Rock around the Clock" as the beginning of rock and roll. If you dig deeper, there are other songs such as "Rocket 88" or "Good Rockin' Tonight" that were the predecessors. While it is a historical fact these songs were recorded before

Elvis entered Sun Studios that fateful day to record "That's Alright Mama," these songs didn't achieve the kind of impact that happened when Elvis appeared. Little Richard and Chuck Berry should be as rich as Bill Gates for the contribution they made to American culture, but it didn't work out that way. Life has always been unfair and it will always be unfair. What made Elvis happen was a combination of his persistence, his incredible voice, his personality on and off stage, extremely fortunate timing, and a whole lot of luck. While even the most diehard Blues Brothers fans, (and I'm sure John Belushi and Dan Ackroyd themselves) would defend the quality of their vocals, it's just sour grapes to say that they didn't have a huge impact on the last thirty years of blues and R & B music. Their love of the art form and the celebrity status at the time gave them the opportunity to make the film and the album that gave the blues a face and made it accessible to the masses. While I'm sure they were as surprised as anybody, the fallout from the film was beneficial to a huge portion of truly American music. It breathed new life into artists like Ray Charles, James Brown, Wilson Pickett, B. B. King, Solomon Burke, Delbert McClinton and hundreds of others. Of course, these artists didn't need anybody's help to convince people of their greatness. But at the time, they were great to a very small number of blues listeners and other purists. *The Blues Brothers* film exposed their music to the masses. I guess even a legendary talent needs a helping hand sometimes. A great song is still a great song even if you're sick of performing it. While James Brown must certainly be sick of "I Feel Good" and B. B. King must be sick to death of "Thrill Is Gone," they continue to do these songs because they know that's what the people want to hear. They acknowledge the fact that these are the songs that brought you to them. I'm confident they would far prefer to be in the position of being sick of a song they have to sing for forty years as opposed to having a bunch of great songs that only a few people want to hear. It's a good problem to have.

As a player who performs songs staple songs like "Mustang Sally" and "Brown Eyed Girl," (for the record, I only sing "Mustang Sally" inside the middle of "Funky Broadway" when I perform with Mick Sterling and the Stud Brothers, for no obvious reason other than it just worked out that way), you have a tendency to take these songs for granted. This was never clearer to me than when I performed at B. B. King's in Memphis in 1998.

I was handed some information from a family friend about a blues festival called Bluestock. It was a multiple day blues festival that featured hundreds of bands from around the country. The goal was to showcase the majority of these bands for industry insiders, A & R people, media, songwriters, publishing companies, etc. They had workshops, trade shows, and other things happening during the day.

The goal of this festival for working bands was similar to all festivals of this kind, to further your career. I put together material from the band and mailed it in, like I have done many times before. Most of the time the replies had been nonexistent, or our material was rejected because of the amount of submissions already received. About three months after I sent it, I received a phone call from Bluestock, asking us if we wanted to fly to Memphis and perform. I honestly had forgotten that I sent the material so it took me a few seconds to even remember the name of the festival. Somehow, the band was available and willing to go to Memphis to showcase for no pay and money out of pocket to do it. Sometimes you've got to take a shot.

The arrangement was that we had a prime spot on the stage at B. B. King's club on Beale Street in Memphis on the Saturday night of the festival. We were also chosen to perform with festival celebrities, the legendary Steve Cropper and the Memphis Horns. We would do one set of our material and the next set would feature performances by Steve Cropper and the Memphis Horns along with us. There was no time for rehearsal, so it was going to be our band performing classic soul hits that Steve Cropper had either written or contributed musically to, and have the Memphis Horns play with our horn section. It was a thrill to have the opportunity to perform with these guys. I'm sure they weren't looking forward to it, but that was the deal they made with the festival. This business has a remarkable power to force you into doing things you would never do on your own. That night we performed to a full and accepting room at B. B. King's. From the first note, the audience connected with the band. It was great to have new ears hear the band. I never worry about how people will accept the band, it's a powerhouse and it has been for years. A few songs in, the Memphis Horns joined us on stage and we performed a few songs that Wayne Jackson from the Memphis Horns suggested. We had no time to rehearse, so everybody just found out the chords on the fly and off we went. As I sat on the side of the stage, I could tell something very special was happening. It's that mysterious thing that happens when great musicians are doing their thing. A glance, nudge, wink, or any other small movement is required to move the song along, even if the players have never played it before together. There was well over a century of musical experience on that stage. It was a thrill for me.

After a couple of songs of the second set, Steve Cropper joined the band onstage. Steve is a giant in the world of soul. One of the main contributors of the Stax-Volt sound, co-writer with Otis Redding on many songs, and basically, drawing up the musical blueprint on how to play soul guitar, Steve Cropper is an American treasure.

One of the funny things that happened that night was what Steve did when he joined the band onstage. At this particular stage, the music instrument and amplifier company PEAVEY was a contributing sponsor to the event. One of the requirements was that the band must play PEAVEY products, drums, amps, etc. When Steve Cropper saw this, he gave us a look that told us he wanted none of it. He just turned on an amp that was directly behind the visible Peavey amp and played through that. He turned the thing up really loud and it sounded so sweet. What the organizers didn't know couldn't hurt them I guess. Besides, no one was man enough to go up against Steve Cropper, he's a giant of a man musically and physically.

His first song was "Sittin' on the Dock of the Bay." The guitar player for my band, Stephen Morgan, was smiling a lot that night. Everybody in my band was. What was also happening was that Steve Cropper and the Memphis Horns were smiling because they realized they were playing with real players, guys who knew the bag. They probably assumed they would be stuck with a sub-par-blues band from Minneapolis, but that wasn't the case that night. The crowd was jammed at the front of the stage and hanging on every word Steve sang. It was thrilling to hear that distinctive guitar sound we all grew up with coming from a stage we were playing on.

After "Dock of the Bay," I came up to sing "Midnight Hour." Just before we did the song, Steve Cropper acknowledged that just down the street, the great Wilson Pickett was at a particular club. That's all right, no pressure on me though; it was just another night in a club.

After our drummer Bobby Vandell counted it off and we hit the first note of "Midnight Hour" the crowd exploded. As soon as I sang the first line, "I'm gonna wait 'til the midnight hour," I had chills from the top of my head to my toes. I was light-headed and nearly fell over. Here I was singing this classic soul song with Steve Cropper and the Memphis Horns in a crowded bar room and it sounded magnificent. The band rose to the occasion and gave the song its just due. I am in no position to say this about grown men, some older than me, but I was proud of my band that night. To paraphrase Mr. Springsteen, we "proved it all night" in Memphis.

We continued with "Soulman" and a couple of other songs that night. It was magical for us. What it made me realize was how much as players we take for granted songs like "Midnight Hour" and "Soulman." These songs have been played again and again by every VFW band and hotel band for nearly forty years from Canada to Singapore. Because of that, the validity of the song gets downgraded. But when you have the chance to play these songs with the guys who actually contributed to the construction of that sound, it hits you over the head and reminds you why these songs have lasted so long. They last because they are accessible and powerful works of art, as valid as anything purists of any genre can offer up. What makes them stand out more is that the masses identify with them.

"Mustang Sally" and other songs like that will never die. As long as there's the opportunity to sing along with the band and as long as people want to dance in a club, those songs will remain intact and a vital part of the night for any band of that performs songs in this genre of music. Chances are the bands performing those songs aren't thrilled about it. If they do their job right, you'd never know what they feel about the song. You'll never know the soul searching it took to get them to the point of performing these songs each time they play. You shouldn't have to. You just came there to forget about your troubles for a while to drink or dance. It's five or ten minutes of the night for the musician to play the song, so it shouldn't be that big of a deal, but it often is. Once you make the choice to perform any song that has mass acceptance, a price is paid. These are the times when you're a musician that you have to suck it up and do your job.

This was shot at the International Market Square at our first big Heart & Soul show with Jonny Lang and Ipso Facto. I remember changing in the bathroom stall with about five minutes to showtime. I was exhausted and clearly delirious as you can tell from that stupid smile on my face. It was a magical night. We raised a lot of money for Camp Heartland.

Tra-la-la-la-la . . .

Chapter 4

*T*he *building blocks of a song have always,* and will always be, a mystery to me. I assume I'm not alone in that sentiment. The fact that so much money and peoples' livelihoods depend on the creation of something you can't put your hands on, is something short of miraculous and nothing short of fascinating. The song is the pillar of the music business. It's the goal that can be reached daily if you're great at it, weekly if you're good at it, yearly if you should be thinking about another line of work.

The inspiration for a song can happen in countless different ways. Maybe it can come from a glance from a lover or a stranger. Maybe it's a sign you read on the street. Maybe it's a passing reference or phrase that sticks in your brain. Sometimes the path from creation to completion of a song can take fifteen minutes. Sometimes it takes weeks. Great songs have been created on restaurant napkins or seemingly out of thin air, on notepads, placemats, and any kind of paper within reach. My preferred method of lyric writing is completely unromantic, I write on the computer. I'm not proud of it.

A song can begin lyrically. It can begin with a melody that you hum for some unexplained reason. It can be a riff on the instrument of your choosing that finds its way to your hands or lips. The majority of the time, the song begins in a solitary manner. It begins with you and, hopefully, will end with you involved.

A song can take a very indirect route to completion. Parts of them can be scrapped forever or used in another song. When that happens to me, it usually means I ran out of ideas, I'm bored with it, or I can tell it's going to stink. Most of the time, I still need to attempt to finish the song even if I know it's eventual rubbish. If I leave it open-ended, it gnaws away at me. I may never share this song with anybody, but at least I got it out of my system. A song is a gift that comes to you with a potentially hefty price tag. The price you pay differs depending on if you do or don't own that song. If you're in a cover band, the price is playing the songs that other people wrote, again and again, until you're sick to death of them. If it's an original work, it more than likely is something drawn from a personal experience. That means that if your song is hated or, even worse, ignored by the public, it's a bitter pill to swallow. For some reason, you needed that song to come out of you and you needed to share it with people. No matter how your outward demeanor is concerning your songs, I firmly believe that every songwriter truly wants one hundred percent of the people who hear their song to love it, even if they don't normally listen to your kind of music. If they don't love it, there's a piece of you that takes it personally. I know I do. It's completely irrational and there's no reason to expect it, but there it is.

The quality of a song is another huge mystery to me. There are no hard rules that make up a great song. There are the standard markings of a song, the intro, verse, chorus, bridge, solo, etc. If a song were an agreement, the letter of the agreement would be met with those elements included. However, the element that gives the song life is the spirit you bring to it. The emotion, the passion, and how carefully you choose your words to express are key. Those things provide the spirit of the agreement within the song.

I've written some god-awful songs that no one will ever see. If I was smart, I'd burn all the lyrics and any tape that I have of these songs, but I just can't seem to do it. Mainly because I know someone will have a copy of some of these songs somewhere, so they'll never be truly gone. Hopefully those people have forgotten about my ineptness within the song. Lyrically, I've written some crap too. Every songwriter writes songs that should—and do—go nowhere. Those bad songs stick with you. You make a point of never letting anybody see those songs in that form. However, there are times you can take pieces of that lame song you wrote one time and use a piece of it in something better you're working on. It's not quite recycled, since you never used it in the first place. To borrow from Tom Waits, sometimes you just need a "new coat of paint" on some junk in your song-writing closet to have your new song make sense to you.

What defines a great song is completely subjective. One thing that can define your reaction to a song is where you hear it the first time. I remember seeing a film in 1975 or '76 that John Sayles directed and Jeff Goldblum starred in called *Between the Lines.* I was in Seattle with my best friend Erik, visiting his dad. We went to this funky theater one night and saw this film. The film was really cool to us that night. One of the things I remember about that film was that was the first time I had ever seen a band called Southside Johnny and the Asbury Jukes. I fell in love with them and the film. A few years later, I saw the film again and it definitely lost its luster. Nothing about the film, even the footage of Southside Johnny wasn't as strong as I remembered. But the combination of atmosphere, geography, and company increased my acceptance of the film and the music that night.

tra-la-la-la-la . . .

As a songwriter in a band, you really have to depend on the patience and acceptance of your bandmates in order to make your song a reality. As the leader of a band for more than fifteen years, I have contributed many songs. I'm not certain about many things, but one thing I am certain of is that on many of my songs, my band members grinned and bared it from the first rehearsal of the song, to the recording, to each time we performed it live. In any band, it's unrealistic to think that everybody in the band will like your song. It's impossible for them to see it the same way as someone who contributed in the initial creation of it. When a band is presented with a song from another band member, many choices and compromises have to be made for the song to be played or recorded.

If the song comes from someone other than the leader of the band, or someone who doesn't carry a lot of weight within the band, the song has a stronger chance of being disregarded or pushed down the list of priorities. If the song comes from someone who is forceful within the band, it stands a better chance. If it comes from the leader of the band, or the declared "songwriters" in the band, chances are good the song will stand a chance of being rehearsed, played live, and perhaps recorded. The band may begrudgingly do these songs. They may do them because they actually dig the songs, or because they're playing their role in the band and following the lead of the leader of the band. They may also agree to them just to keep their gig. It's best not to think too much about everybody's motivation behind performing your song, just try to get it out there and see how people like it.

All of us hear songs that make us wonder how the artist performing it could actually think it's good enough to put on a record. I've purchased albums with one good song, and the other nine or ten songs are pure filler. The artist who recorded it sure didn't want to make a record with nine or ten filler songs. None of us go in to this business to create filler songs. All songwriters want all of their songs to be fantastic. Most aren't. Even the Beatles had some clunkers every once in a while. As you may expect, the percentage of clunkers happen far more often.

Many local CDs in any town across the nation fall under the category of being released too hastily or without much thought. As someone who has had the opportunity to hear hundreds of bands' CDs for consideration for festivals and nightclubs, this issue defines itself quite often.

On every recorded piece of work, someone in the band thinks what's on the CD is worthy of someone hearing it. Perhaps their friends who know the band members really like the songs on the record or, if they see the band play it live, it will dictate if the bands puts that song on a CD. The problem with that thought process is when someone hears that song with no connection to the band for the first time. You have to ask yourself some questions: Can that song that you and your friends claim as great stand the test of someone hearing it for the first time? Will that song stand out in a sterile setting or with someone going through dozens of songs an hour? Will a critic who listens carefully to hundreds of CDs a month recognize the greatness of your song? Will it stand out? Common sense tells me that most songs released locally can't survive this test.

Back in 1995, I took a couple of trips out to Los Angeles to shop the Mick Sterling and the Stud Brothers CD, called *Come Home*. I flew out there with a music lawyer who was working with us at the time. The intent of this trip was to introduce the band to publishers, record companies, and music industry people. What it wound up being was an all-expenses-paid trip to L. A. for our lawyer and me to spend a few days in the Golden State in February. I'm not sure if anything was really accomplished in either of these trips, but the ocean sure was pretty.

We actually did attend meetings while we were in L. A. We visited the offices of Sony Music, Peer Publishing, and others in the music industry. At all the meetings, the process was the same. As important as these meetings were, I was very calm, probably too calm. I was also very intimidated which, at the time, I knew was a bad idea.

At all of the meetings we would wait for a long while in the lobby to be greeted by the person we were going to see. Eventually, we would enter the office and make our pitch. Sometimes it took ten minutes; sometimes it took an hour. It all depended on the relationship built between my lawyer and this person. If he was meeting them for the first time, it hinged on how well he did with an initial face-to-face. I found myself in the meetings being very quiet and humble. In hindsight, my demeanor was completely wrong for these meetings. Why would anybody want to sign someone who is humble and quiet? I gave them nothing to get excited about.

At all these meetings, we would hand them the CD. This particular CD we were shopping was a live CD. Again, in hindsight it was a real bonehead move. Outside of *Frampton Comes Alive, Live at Budokan* by Cheap Trick, and the Allman Brothers' *Live at the Fillmore,* the overwhelming majority of live records have not really done anything. At least those bands already had a deal and released studio CDs leading up to their live CD. We did too, but only our fans in Minneapolis knew about them. What would lead me to think that someone's going to get excited about a live CD done by a band from the Midwest? My crystal clear vision that I thought I had for these trips wound up being pretty cloudy. I was ill prepared in so many ways.

At the vast majority of the meetings I had in L. A., the person we were seeing would not listen to the CD in front of us.

Many times, it was obvious they were eager to find a reason to end the meeting. At the time, I was hoping that they would listen to it later. I tried to silence that little voice in my head telling me there wasn't a chance in hell they would listen to my stuff. My little voice was right of course. I can hear the thud of the CD being thrown in their $100 metal waste box under their desk as I'm writing this. It was a hard lesson to learn. It doesn't have to be that way though.

For any band that's ready and willing to take the next step to further its career, it's essential that you have a plan and an understanding of how you present yourself and who is representing you. Our lawyer wore black jeans, a funky old hat, and black nail polish. This is how he walked into our meetings in L. A. Since my band was paying for his trip to L. A., I should have insisted that he wear a suit, take the hat off, and at minimum, wear a lighter shade of color on his fingers. Many times, meetings were made on the fly instead of having meetings set in stone before we arrived. At the minimum, the meetings should have been made the day before, at the maximum, weeks before. That didn't happen on our trips. Many times, we just drove around L. A., hung out at Venice Beach, walked the Santa Monica Pier, and talked about all of the things that could happen if someone liked the CD. It was enjoyable, but unproductive.

The reality was, meetings happened, we schmoozed, we handed out a bunch of CDs, and all I could hear was the thud. The thud of wasted trips and money. The thud of the realization of a severe lack of preparation on my part. The thud of realizing that there was nothing special enough on our live CD that could possibly interest someone in L. A. who had never seen the band, or heard of me before. It was a humbling experience. It's a humbling business and it always will be no matter how successful you may be.

While I'm very proud of all the songs that were on that record, there wasn't a chance in hell that one of them was special enough to stop traffic. I knew it then, I chose to ignore it and believe in sweeter things. I convinced myself that if I presented myself as humble and easy to get along with, L. A. would like me. If I met these people at a party and acted like that, maybe they would. That wasn't where I was meeting them. I met them at their place of business. They're in the business to make money. When I entered their office, their first thought is, and should be: How can I make money off this guy?

In the music business, you don't make money off someone who is too shy and humble, pitching a live CD of a ten-piece band from the Midwest. You make money with someone who attracts your attention musically and visually. I was offering neither one of those enticements.

As a bandleader I didn't represent my band properly in L. A. I didn't have the foresight to realize what was needed. I didn't have the fortitude to insist on things that, in my gut, I knew needed to be done. I put my faith in someone who I barely knew. I deferred to his knowledge about the music business. To borrow an old phrase, I was viewing the entire process through rose-colored glasses. Someone should have slapped some sense into me. It probably wouldn't have worked. I had stars in my eyes. Just another dreamer in Hollywood, if only for a couple of weeks.

While I enjoyed traveling to L. A., there was no way that I, or the band, could have delivered if we were called to accept the task of taking the band to the next level. I had a wife and two small children who I would have missed terribly. Each member of my band was performing too much in town. It would have taken an enormous change in attitude to turn into a touring band to promote a CD. At the time, the decision to pay a lawyer was very controversial. If someone would have bit on us and signed us, it would have tore the band apart as it was. We were in no position to make that dramatic change.

As spontaneous and creative as this business is, it's still based on the bedrock of business principles. Planning, preparation, reality checks, how you conduct yourself with others, and basically the ability to deliver the goods will decide your fate. If you're a local band or solo artist, it's always good take a step back and think about all of the ramifications of your decision to take your career to the next level. Do you want to change your life that much? Do you want to be on the road for a long time? Can you afford it? Are you confident in your ability to think that people in other cities, total strangers, will dig your stuff? If you have a spouse and kids at home, is being on the road making $60 a night and spending ten hours in the van traveling to the next gig worth it for you? In the end, are your songs so good that total strangers will love it the first time they hear it?

I've written far more bad songs than good ones. I'm sure that's the percentage for all songwriters. I'll continue to write songs simply because it's what I do. Hopefully people will like them. I can only go by my own barometer. If it moves me, I can make a song work. How far that song gets depends on how far I want that song to go and in finding the right outlets and people to get it there. The longer I write, the more I think I have a better perspective of what should be released and what needs more work or what shouldn't see the light of day. Local bands would serve themselves well if they edited more of their songs before they release something. If they want to make the step to the next level, they have to get out of the frame of mind, depending on their friends, loved ones, or even their fan base to judge if a song is good. Don't get me wrong, that helps, but it takes more than that. It only takes one song to spark interest. Make that one song stand out. Take time with it. Work out the kinks. Make it shine and it may stand a chance.

la-la-la-la-la . . .

One of the least favorite things for my band is to take the dreaded
"group photo." We avoid it as much as we can. This was shot by the
extremely patient photographer, Tom Asp, between sets at Bunkers one
night. As you can tell, there are mixed emotions about the process.
From left, back row: Bob Hallgrimson—Trumpet, Stephen Morgan—
Guitar, Nick Salisbury—Bass, Donnie LaMarca—Piano, me in the hat;
From left, front row: Pat Mackin—Sax, King Steven Pikal—Trombone,
Ronny Loew—Sax, Bobby Vandell—Drums, Mark Lickteig—
Hammond Organ and Vocals

Intro, verse, chorus, verse, chorus, solo, bridge, chorus out

eing in a band is very hard work. The common theme among local musicians is to find some way to cover the nut. How much can you get paid from the gig to get you to the next gig? Can you make enough from gigs to make your house payment? How many ways do you have to split what the club pays you? How much for the agent fee? And much more. When you're in the thick of just trying to keep your gig, you have to focus on so many short-term solutions. Unfortunately for most musicians, they wind up continually chasing the quick fix of searching for a higher paid gig, they look past the one way they can make some real money in this business.

I'm guilty of negligence when it comes to this aspect of the music business. I've never seriously pursued focusing on becoming a songwriter as a way to earn extra income. I focus on writing songs for my self-released CDs and hope that my audience likes it enough to buy the CD. I suppose it's getting over the hurdle of convincing myself that songs I play a role in creating would interest another artist enough to cover them. I like and get them, but will someone else see the worth in it? While song writing can be very lucrative, mostly it's just such a long and subjective way to make a living.

For me, it's always been about what my paycheck looks like at the end of the week to pay my bills. That's been my priority because it had to be. If I would have had some tenacity, faith and belief in my song-writing abilities, maybe my musical career would have been broader in scope.

The majority of the time, the hats songwriters and performers wear are two different things. If you can juggle both, your chances improve on eventually being successful in the music business. If you can't, musicians either focus on one thing or the other. If you make the transition from depending on live performances for your income to counting on your songs to feed your family, it could be very tough, pride swallowing, and humbling. It requires you to censor your urge to force the artist doing your song to do it the way you want it done.

In effect, a professional songwriter has to regularly give away his musical version of his children when they finish a song. In the end, it requires a lot of trust and faith from creation to completion of the process. Being a songwriter means you have to get used to being rejected, critiqued, minimized, taken for granted, expected to change your ideas immediately and like it, and expected to be the artist's best friend and confidant at any moment. Sounds like fun doesn't it?

Twin City native Kevin Bowe is someone who has made the transition from focusing on live performances to becoming a full-time songwriter and producer. He was the first artist in more than twenty years to be signed by song-writing giants Jerry Leiber and Mike Stoller. Kevin's work includes songs that have appeared on Grammy-Award-winning records and W. C. Handy Award winners as well. You can hear Kevin's work on the first two CDs from Jonny Lang, as well Delbert McClinton, Etta James, The Proclaimers, John Mayall, Lynyrd Skynrd, Three Dog Night, and Leo Kottke, among many others. His songs have been featured in multiple film soundtracks and television shows. His producing credits include Blind Pig recording artists Renee Austin and Shanachie artist Shane Henry, as well as national Blues artist Tommy Castro, to name a few. He has released five of his own CDs, *Blackie Ford's Revenge, Restoration, Love Songs and Murder Ballads, Angels on the Freeway,* and *Doin' it for the People.* Kevin still performs in the Twin Cities with his own band, the Okemah Prophets. He also performs with me quite often in a band we call The Rolling Blunder Revue. Kevin is in the position to perform when he wants to, not because he needs to. His primary source of income is his song writing and producing. Coming to that point in a musician's professional life can be liberating. It can also be a very tough financial road to go down.

Kevin and I have haunted similar clubs and studios off and on for the past twenty years. However, our paths rarely crossed. When they did, it was just a wave and a glance. In 1998, I asked Kevin to contribute his song, "Sweeter World," to a compilation CD I was producing for Camp Heartland, a place for kids living with HIV/AIDS. It was part of the fundraising effort I created called Heart & Soul. In late 1998, I asked Kevin for a demo tape of some of his songs for an upcoming CD I was working on. He sent me a cassette of nearly twenty songs. Three songs really connected with me, "Honey Honey Honey," "The Day it Comes," and "Blues Is My Business." It was a good shot in the arm for me to hear those songs. They gave me some inspiration for the eventual completion of the record.

We both thought it was important to write a couple of new songs together. So in late 1998 and on New Years Day 1999, Kevin and I got together to write. What resulted were the songs "Soul of a Woman" and "Someone's Waiting for Me at Home," two of my favorite songs I've been involved in. It was also the first time that I had written lyrics with someone in the same room at the same time. It was obvious to me that Kevin knew the give and take of collaboration and how to get results.

Since then, we've worked together on a live CD called *Doin' It for the People,* as well as playing many gigs in coffee houses, clubs, private parties, and outdoor events with our band, The Rolling Blunder Revue. Because of his involvement in the Blunders, juggling his live duties and song-writing duties can become chaotic. What separates Kevin from others in this position is that he's put the years in and he has a track record strong enough to know when to put the brakes on the live shows and focus on his song-writing and producing duties. Because of Pro-Tools digital recording software and e-mail, songwriters can create what they want to express in the comfort of their own home.

Communication and delivery of the songs can be done via e-mail. While making a living being a songwriter is never easy, technology has provided far better tools to create songs than ever before.

If you write a song and you want to get it out there, what do you do? If you just send your song to an artist or publisher out of the blue, the chances are very good your song will wind up in a wastebasket. If you expect a publisher to find you by word of mouth because you write such amazing songs, you may be waiting for a long time. You can hire someone to get your songs to a publisher or artist, but that can be costly and the results will more than likely be disappointing to you. Sometimes you have to just handle things on your own, at least initially, to get your songs out there.

"I saw the name 'Bug Music' on the back of John Hiatt's *Bring the Family* record, and called long distance information for the phone number," recalled Bowe. His opening remarks to them were as simple as this, "I want to work with you guys." From the opening conversation, Kevin made arrangements to send his material to Bug Music and a relationship began.

In 1995, Bowe scored his first major song placement on the Kenny Wayne Shepherd CD, *Ledbetter Heights* with a song called "Riverside." During this same time, he found himself in Fargo, North Dakota, one night and came across a thirteen-year-old kid who had been playing guitar for nine months and was creating a buzz in town. This kid's name was Jonny Lang. As Jonny's career progressed, his live shows were creating significant buzz and it became clear that Jonny was destined for bigger things than playing club land.

"I introduced Jonny to James Klein of Blue Sky Management in Minneapolis and called my pal David Z, recommending that David produce some songs with him. Jonny and I worked on two CDs together, cowriting several songs and both CDs went platinum" said Kevin.

The Gods of Fargo struck again with another young phenom by the name of Shannon Curfman. I learned about Shannon from a local news story. Because of the buzz concerning Jonny, the time was ripe for another young artist to emerge. The fact that it was a young girl, and she was from Fargo, just made the story even more incredible. Both Bowe and I played a role in Shannon's quick rise to notoriety. Bowe's role was far more instrumental in her success. My role was in the early stages.

After seeing the story on TV, I contacted Shannon and her mother. My initial intent was to ask them to perform at the Heart & Soul concert series I was producing. Since the event was for kids and Shannon was still just a kid—a very talented and gifted kid—it seemed like a good fit.

We agreed to meet at one of the glamour spots of Minneapolis where all the big deals get done, the Embers restaurant on Interstate 394 in Golden Valley. I met Shannon, her mother, and her father. I had the brilliant idea during that meeting to explore the possibility of managing Shannon. In

Intro, verse, chorus, verse, chorus, solo, bridge, chorus out

theory, it seemed like a good fit. They were new in town, they needed support. I could provide them a showcase with Heart & Soul and help them mold the sound of her band at the time. Her talent was obvious and the timing was good considering the success of Jonny Lang.

What followed were many meetings with Shannon and her mom, as well as seeing her perform live. My managing partner, Mara Jacob, and I set up some Tuesday nights at Bunkers with another rising female artist, Renee Austin. It was at these shows that we critiqued Shannon and her band. It was obvious to us (and, I suspect, her band) that the band was eventually going to be replaced. Shannon was the focus. The reaction of the crowd to such a young girl singing and playing the guitar like she did was as we expected.

What we were attempting to do was work out the kinks in what she was doing to take her to the next level. Each week that she performed, other industry people working in Minneapolis were coming into the club to check her out. We knew there was intense interest in Shannon from many parties. Lots of rumors were going around. The biggest one was that Shannon was going to make a move, and we weren't going to be involved. As soon as we saw Jonny Lang's dad at the club, I knew which way the wind was blowing and it was blowing up the wrong skirt.

We couldn't compete with the possibility of management by Jonny Lang's dad. Jonny had taken a special interest in Shannon. They were Fargo natives. Their stories were similar. She wanted to be associated with the Lang family. The writing was on the wall.

I wasn't too surprised when we received the news from Shannon and her mom that they were going with them. In hindsight, it was a blessing. I was still too focused on trying to get myself a record deal. I didn't have the time or the dedication needed to manage someone. Even though the timing was remarkable for Shannon and the probability of attaining a record deal for her was clearly within reach, she was still thirteen years old. I already had two kids to take care of, did I need to watch over another one? Was taking on this huge responsibility worth being gone so much from my family? In hindsight, it wasn't. But if it did go down like I wanted it to, I probably would have ridden the wave and dealt with the hassles that all managers have with adult artists, let alone, a teenager's hassles. I'm glad it slipped away from me. My intent at the time was to take this opportunity to maybe take my career in a new direction. In reality, the reason this didn't work out was because I was dishonest with myself. I was doing it for the wrong reasons. I should have listened to my gut instead of dreaming that the numbers in my checking account would grow because of this young girl.

Eventually, Shannon Curfman hooked up with Tom Tucker from Master Mix studios in Minneapolis and later wound up with another management change to Jake Walesch, a strong and savvy manager in the Twin Cities area. Through the course of all these changes, Bowe was introduced to Shannon and they started writing songs for an upcoming CD under the watchful eye of legendary Clive Davis. Bowe had multiple songs on her record. Shannon was heavily promoted by the Clive Davis promotional machine. She toured the country, showed up on TV shows and got favorable reviews. Playing a significant role in Shannon's record was another stepping stone for Bowe's songwriting career.

One of the trade-offs that songwriters go through in order to get their songs out there is to sometime share an inordinate percentage of the writing credit with the artist. This can happen with established artists, or new artists that the label is hot on. This can happen despite the fact that the artist barely contributes anything (or nothing at all) to the creation of the song. At times,

Intro, verse, chorus, verse, chorus, solo, bridge, chorus out

the songwriter has to give up half of the ownership of the song, just so the song can get placed on a recording. If you're thinking of your song-writing career in broad strokes, giving up a little could eventually benefit you in a larger way.

The more places your songs start showing up, the more opportunity you have to get in front of other artists in need of material. Because of the success of Bowe's songs with Jonny, Shannon, Kenny Wayne, and placements on various film and TV shows, Kevin was able to get more of his songs on releases from new artists, as well as established artists. How you deal with a new artist comes with his or her own set of issues. Writing with artists who have decades of success in the business can be intimidating. "Each one is different," says Bowe, "and sometimes you don't get to know them well enough to get close to eccentricities. Usually with the long timers, they're such pros that it's all about the song. The rest of the time is spent trading bizarre stories about our histories in the biz."

One of Kevin's recent efforts was with the legendary soul singer, Etta James. Their working relationship began with a phone call from Etta herself. "I was sitting on my butt in Minneapolis when the phone rang," says Bowe. "I had gotten a call from a pal who was producing Etta's album and he had asked me to send him some songs. I had done that months earlier, having no expectations of hearing anything further about it. Eventually, he called and actually put Etta on the phone. She was very enthusiastic and funny, wanting to know where I'd been all her life, etc. She asked me if I was a white boy (I told her, not anymore!). She cut four of my songs and we talked on the phone several times." To make it even sweeter, Etta called again on Bowe, this time, at a concert. "I finally got to visit her when she did a gig at the Guthrie Theater in Minneapolis," recalls Bowe. "She called me out from the stage. I went to see her after the show, took pictures, etc. When the album won the Best Contemporary Blues Grammy, I called her to congratulate her, and she was pretty happy about the whole thing, as was I."

Fame and glory for all of us are fleeting, even for someone finding out they just played a large role in a Grammy Award-winning project. Bowe simply stated this workman-like response, "Then I got up the next day and went back to work in the basement!" It's a glamorous business. Just because you have a publisher, doesn't mean you can sit back and expect them to place your songs. As with any job, the only person you can count on for your own success is you. "No publisher has ever gotten any of my songs used in any way whatsoever. I've had to do it myself, which is common. My TV and film placements have been assisted by a woman in the business who puts my songs in front of music supervisors of the specific project," says Bowe. One of Bowe's biggest song placements was on *The Sopranos* with a song he cowrote with Nashville songwriter Todd Cerney, "Blues Is My Business (and Business Is Good)."

Many times the route a song takes to be placed in a film or TV show goes through many filters. The song "Blues Is My Business" was no different. "The song had been cut by Etta James on her *Let's Roll* album and it won the Grammy for Best Contemporary Blues Recording," says Bowe. "So a lot of people ended up hearing it. One of those happened to be the music supervisor for *The Sopranos,* whose job it is to find and get clearance for all music used on the show. She picked the song to be run over the end credits for a particularly lovely and violent episode! She then contacted Windswept Pacific, which had purchased Leiber & Stoller Music—the company I had been signed to when I wrote the song. Windswept basically owns twenty five percent of my half of the song (I cowrote it with Todd Cerney in Nashville, who came up with the song's title). The music supervisor made an offer to Windswept. Windswept said yes, and that was that.

"It was a particularly good placement because it's a popular show and the fact that they used the song over the end credits means that it played very loud for a long period of time, which means it pays more on the performance royalties as well as on the initial fee. Performance royalties are collected by BMI. Every time the episode airs, the network has to pay BMI more money, which eventually trickles down to the writers. It is important to point out that as with about 98 percent of my income from song writing, none of the revenue was generated by the actions of a publisher. In my experience, all of my cuts on other people's albums and all of my film/TV uses have either come from a random call like this or from my own efforts."

As with anything, the more you work on something, the chances improve of you becoming better at it. Song writing is no different. What makes this profession different from others in the business world is that the success of your work depends on gut-level reactions. People ranging from supposed experts in the business, other musicians, music critics and other fringe employees in the music business will decide your fate. Despite that, if you've got the stomach, the patience, the organizational skills, and most importantly, you can write a song worth listening to, it's worth the effort.

Words of advice and unwelcome advice will come to you fast and furious throughout your process. You have the choice to listen or ignore it. The jury is still out if you will succeed or fail by following either path. Bob Dylan said, "Trust yourself, so you won't be disappointed when the people let you down." Bowe describes it this way, "Listen to your heroes and steal as much as you can. Write as much as possible. Judge yourself harshly but not so much that you get too discouraged to do it. Cowrite with people who are better than you. Don't just write about yourself or things you know. Use your imagination and remember what Picasso said . . . 'Art is the lie that tells the truth.'"

Intro, verse, chorus, verse, chorus, solo, bridge, chorus out

My apologies to Marc Norberg for this beat up old proof sheet. Marc has shot some of the greatest blues and soul artists in the world, and his photos are flawless. I just loved the flow of this proof sheet. It illustrates perfectly how fortunate I've been to be married to Kristi.

Are you with the band?

Chapter 6

*O*ne of the toughest things about being in a relationship with any musician who performs in venues from VFW Halls and clubs to theaters and stadiums is the fact that they will never belong to you completely. For some reason, there's something about someone performing that makes the person on stage a bit more attractive to the opposite sex. The combination of the lights, the music, and the actual size of the stage just naturally sets them apart from the guy who stinks of strawberry-flavored Swisher Sweets and gin while he hits on you. The actual venue doesn't seem to matter. If a musician is doing his or her thing, there's a good chance that someone is attracted to him or her. How they act upon that attraction is one thing, but the attraction is there nonetheless. When someone is in love with a musician, the majority of the time, the initial spark that started their relationship involved music. Most of the time, it involved seeing the object of your love doing what he or she does for a living, playing music live. How a relationship survives the unusual nature of being in love with a musician can have dozens of perfectly rational psychological explanations that would apply. In the end, it really gets down to this: if you're with someone who gets it, really gets it, chances are the relationship will work. If not, it could get ugly quickly, or slowly, which may be worse.

I've never had a relationship with a woman in a band, so for the sake of simplicity for the rest of this chapter, (and no offense meant to women musicians by any means), the cast of characters will read like this: Musician—man, and Woman—wife or girlfriend. It's not a sexist thing. I'm not saying a woman musician is weaker or less than a male musician; some of my favorite records are from women artists, it's just that I have no idea what a man goes through dating or marrying a woman musician. So please, no hate mail. Women know everything and they always will. These are just very general observations are from a man's point of view.

When a woman starts going out with a musician, you can count on a few basic things to happen. You'll see the girlfriend at nearly all of his gigs. The girlfriend will most likely introduce herself to the rest of the band and become friends. The other band members' girlfriends will introduce themselves to the new girlfriend. The band girlfriends start hanging out together at the gig, sitting at the same table. People who see the band a lot start wanting to find out about the band girlfriends and then they start to become friends with the girlfriends and, in turn, the band itself.

At this table, words are exchanged that are not decipherable from the stage while the band is playing. Exactly what they're all saying is something you may or may not find out later. Another element of the girlfriend table is the palpable force field that surrounds the table. This is an important table and one that shouldn't be messed with by other men or women. If you're a guy, hanging out at this table will draw suspicious stares from the band members. If the guy asks the standard question of any band girlfriend, "Are you with the band?" he runs the risk of getting an answer he doesn't want to hear, delivered politely or rudely. If you're a woman going up to this table, staring at one of the band members, you run the risk of ridicule and mockery delivered straight to your face or directly to your back as you walk away. Man or woman has to follow some basic rules of the girlfriend table. Don't knock the table. Don't dance too close to the table. Don't knock over the drinks. Don't block the sightline to the stage. Mostly, follow the etiquette of "the table" and everything will be hunky dory. That's just the rules of the table. Now, on to the ninety-seven other things you have to worry about.

The bottom line is, when a woman begins a relationship with a musician, it just seems to be far more intense than with someone in another profession. Hard to tell exactly the source of the intensity; all I know is, it's there. Eventually, as with any new relationship, the things that initially turned you on about the guy become more commonplace. Often, you see that in the form of the amount of gigs the girlfriend or wife go to start dwindling. It may not be due to the relationship burning out, it may simply be that she's bored seeing you play every night. Honestly, who can blame them? There's not a man alive who would watch his girlfriend work every night, doing basically the same thing for five hours. Why should a woman have the patience for it after a while?

Also, the people at the band table are growing predictable. The same people in the bar come up to you and ask about your boyfriend or husband. They've heard the same songs and set list. They still think you're good at what you do, they just don't feel the need to see you perform as often. This is when the blooms start falling off the petal. Does the guy who leaves the toilet seat up, leaves his clothes all over your place, snores, has morning breath, is often broke, and now his job is starting to become boring, still do it for you?

The intensity of a relationship is something that band members can spot a mile away. The demeanor of a new girlfriend at a gig is normally a positive one. Lots of laughter, lots of smiles to the boyfriend on stage. Lots of holding each other between sets. Sometimes the girlfriend will help her man load some of his gear after the gig. Once things settle down a bit, band members start seeing less of the girlfriend. When they do see the girlfriend again, she may seem happy to be there, but the smiles are less frequent. She's looking at her watch more during your gigs. There are other things she could be—and probably should be—doing. When you come home from the gig, instead of your girlfriend or wife waiting up for you, she's asleep and doesn't want to be woken up like she used to. It may be due to the fact she's not digging you as much as she used to. But it also may mean that she needs to wake up in the morning and you don't have to wake up until two in the afternoon. What also may be happening is that the initial attraction and lust that instigated everything just isn't cutting it anymore. How deeply does she want to become involved with a musician?

A new relationship means that your girlfriend will most likely ask all of her friends to come and see you play. After a while (and contingent on how good you actually are), the amount of friends who continue to see you will add or subtract pretty quickly. As a musician, you don't want your girlfriend or wife to see you in a club that sucks or has a lame vibe to it. It's hard enough to do those gigs without people you know actually seeing you. Playing those kinds of gigs is hard enough. When someone knows you at those gigs, it's humiliating and embarrassing. When the woman you're with sees you in those kinds of gigs, it just seems natural to me that the level of respect she has for you has to diminish, even if she doesn't say it to your face. How couldn't it? Mine would for her, as much as I wouldn't want it to.

I don't know what a girlfriend or wife of a stockbroker or a boat salesman goes through. The boat salesmen and stockbrokers must be passionate about what they do, but is it the same kind of passion as a musician? I tend to doubt it. I'm guessing the initial attraction wasn't as strong as a woman seeing a musician play on stage. It can be a hell of a lot of fun going out with a musician I suppose. Lots of laughs, free stuff, hanging out with other musicians, etc. But the behind-the-scenes stuff, the jealousy, envy, lack of money, and trying to actually see each other occasionally must get old for the non-musician in the relationship. When this starts happening in a relationship, the musician has to ask himself the questions he's been avoiding because he hates conflict, he's too busy to deal with it, he's too stupid to realize it, or the sex is fantastic enough to look past it. Does she really get what you do? Do you really want her to get it in the first place? She must have been able to get you at one time.

The trick is finding someone who will continue to understand and support what you're doing. That doesn't mean she should hold your hand as you jump off a bridge of stupidity. The trick is finding a woman who has a strong stomach for absurdity and the patience of a saint. If she continues to love you through all of it, that's a bonus. If she's hot twenty-five years later, and she still loves you despite your display of God's cruel joke of a much larger forehead and unwanted ear and back hair, double bonus.

The first and, thankfully, last instance of a relationship merging with my singing career happened in 1983 when my junior high crush, Kristi Knutson, showed up at Bunkers one night to see my band play. Seeing Kristi again brought back many fond and terrifying moments for me that night.

In ninth grade, I attended Plymouth Junior High School in Plymouth. I was in my last year at Plymouth. I'd survived the hell that was seventh grade. I found some kind of groove in eighth grade. By ninth grade, I was feeling comfortable in my own skin, as much as any ninth grade boy with raging uncontrollable hormones can. The past two years, I was one of the lead characters for the musicals at both nearby high schools, Cooper and Armstrong. At that time, the community heavily attended the high school musicals. So the fact that I had been one of the lead players in these shows did not go unnoticed by the drama teacher at Plymouth. It was a good thing too. Because without him asking me to come to an audition, my life as it stands today would be completely different.

During the first month of ninth grade, an audition was being held for an improvisational group called Soup Group. The director of the group, Ert Hermerding, was a graduate of Augsburg College in Minneapolis. He was also a big fan of the critically praised and influential Dudley Riggs' Brave New Workshop, also based in Minneapolis. Ert brought that concept to Plymouth Junior High. I'd never seen their shows when I was in seventh and eighth grade, but I heard about them. To be in this group was considered to be a great thing. I wanted in. I'd done musicals before, but I'd never done any type of improvisational theater. I considered it a challenge. Little did I know that my biggest challenge the day of the audition was to try and contain my teenage lust.

The audition room was filled with teenagers. The method of the audition was for each person to sing one song and some type of monologue in front of all the people auditioning. As you can imagine, some of the auditions were angst, panic ridden nightmares for both the person auditioning and the audience having to sit through it. Everybody was really supportive, but when something sucks, it generally sucks and everyone knows it.

I don't remember what my monologue was, but I do remember I sang the Elton John song "Burn Down the

Mission" with my friend Annie Miners accompanying me. I felt I did a good job and the audience sure liked it. A few kids later, this girl walked up to the stage and every boy in the room immediately got stupid. Her name was Kristi Knutson. She had just moved from Cloquet, Minnesota. I can't believe I hadn't seen her in school yet considering what I was looking at on stage. To say that this girl stood out from all the other girls at my school was an understatement. Every boy in that room was thinking many things, but the universal thought was, God bless Levi Strauss. This chick knew how to wear jeans. Kristi stood up on stage and proceeded to sing her song.

She leaned against the blackboard and started sing "I am stuck on Band-Aids, 'cause Band-Aids' stuck on me." That song never sounded so glorious. She also had this combination of twang and lisp that was something I'd never heard before. The package of Kristi, the jeans, the song, the twang, the body, and the smile just about put me over the edge. Even though her song wasn't the most produced song in the room, it certainly did the trick. She was special, and everyone knew it.

My attraction to her was immediate. The intimidation factor concerning Kristi Knutson would last through all the shows that year, and for many years to come. Because of the show, Kristi and I had many mutual friends. The difference was all of her friends were copying damn near everything she wore and did. Kristi hung out with the popular kids in ninth grade. I knew all of them and I had my own respectable clique going on, but it wasn't in the same league as Kristi. Through these years, Kristi and I would be cordial to each other. I loved seeing her, but she was so damn beautiful that I just couldn't get it together to have a conversation of any substance with her.

Ninth grade was also the time that the "Top Ten" list began. Mike Larson, my best friend Erik Elias, and I came up with the concept. This list was a sacred list and as tough to enter as

Studio 54 was back in the day. This list consisted of the hottest girls in Plymouth. Some girls made an impression in this list and lasted a couple of weeks. Some lasted longer. There were some hot girls in Plymouth, and we gave them their due. But only one name was always in the Top Ten, one name that had staying power. That name was Kristi Knutson. Pathetic, I know. Cut me some slack, I was in the ninth grade.

As we entered high school, Kristi and I found ourselves working at the local Perkins Restaurant in Golden Valley, Minnesota. At the time, this Perkins was considered a hot spot for kids going to Armstrong High School. Getting a job at Perkins was a good gig back then. Kristi and I worked the weekend bar rush shift, ten at night to six in the morning every Friday and Saturday. This shift was entertaining for many reasons. Drunks would come in. Rowdy and unruly groups ordered French fries and pancakes and unlimited pots of coffee. The lobby was always filled. Friends would come in and talk to you during your shift. It was a melting pot of freaks, jocks, audio visual nerds, punks, and Goths (that term wasn't invented back then, but believe me, today's punks and Goths have nothing on the '70s crew). Every weekend night, it was a gossip-filled, apricot-syrup-ignoring, tub of intrigue with the scent of buttermilk pancakes numbing our senses. For some unknown reason, Kristi was the only girl I knew who could make those horrendous Perkins waitress outfits actually look good. That's a gift. We loved working at Perkins. The tips were great, and we got to sleep all day after the shift.

The summer Kristi and I worked at Perkins, we found ourselves at a party thrown at my friend Annie's house. Annie's house was one of the destinations for any house party. Some houses are built like that, they seem to accept kids better than others. Annie threw a great party too. Her parents never minded, they had basically moved all their stuff downstairs in their converted basement and lived there. The party was inside Annie's house and in her backyard. My house was a block away from Annie's. I would cut through a couple of yards to make my trip even shorter. That night, as I walked to Annie's backyard, I saw Kristi. For some reason that night, I was able to hold a conversation with her. It was going really well. We seemed to focus on each other that night. Lots of laughs, great music, beautiful summer night, this was good stuff. As it got to be around one in the morning, I decided that I'd better get home. Kristi offered to give me a ride to my house. I told her that I lived a block away, but she still insisted. So Kristi drove one minute and brought me to my driveway. We started talking some more and all of a sudden we started kissing, then we kissed some more. This was heavy. My mind was blown. I was kissing Kristi Knutson in my driveway. What the hell was going on? I'm not sure how long we made out in my driveway that night, but I do remember that it was spectacular. We both made jokes about how surprised everyone would be. Eventually, I got out of the car and Kristi drove away. Just then, I did what every boy does after he makes out with a girl, I called my best friend Erik and told him that KRISTI KNUTSON just made out with me! The girl with the longest record on our sacred Top Ten list had just made out with me, of all people. Erik and I were laughing hysterically. This kind of stuff didn't happen to kids like me. But it happened that night. I loved that night.

After our first make-out session, Kristi and I went on a couple of dates that summer. This should have been a glorious time for me. I had nothing to be intimidated about anymore. She liked me. Unfortunately, my suspicious nature took hold. Why is she going out with me? Why is she agreeing to kiss me at anytime? When do I get dumped? Is this some kind of joke she's playing on me? When are her friends going to openly mock me? Stuff like that. Needless to say, my dates with Kristi back then didn't go as well as they could have. I intimidated myself out of having a relationship.

Somehow through my unique ability to fumble and sweat around her, Kristi and I remained friends. Our paths crossed occasionally throughout high school, but our summer romance never repeated itself. After we graduated, I rarely saw Kristi. My old friends Annie Miners, Peter Guertin, and Shannon Jewett and I eventually rented a house in North Minneapolis for a while. The happenings of that house would keep a psychiatrist in business for many years and worthy of a two-thousand-page opus. However, one of the great things that did happen in that house was a continuation of what had happened at Annie's house when we were teenagers. We had a piano. Peter would play, and we would sing. It was what our house in North Minneapolis was known for. Kristi came over one night while we were at the house, just prior to moving to St. Louis to work for a cable station doing producing and on-air duties. She was nineteen.

While Kristi was in St. Louis, I was performing in bands that didn't amount to much. Lots of fun was had, but nothing significant musically. We worked hard, but never attracted a following. One night while I was playing at Bunkers with the band Heat Treatment, I saw Kristi in the audience. She had just moved back from St. Louis a few days earlier. It was great to see her. We talked after the set. It was clear that things had changed. I was far more comfortable with her than I used to be in high school. As a matter of fact, the roles had reversed. I wasn't so insecure anymore and she noticed that. As I left that night, I was hoping I would see her again soon. I did. Since we had mutual friends, word was starting to get out that Kristi was interested in me. I was always interested in her, but it was more of a pipe dream than a possibility. But things had changed. It could have been a combination of her being homesick and feeling relieved to actually be home. Whatever it was, seeing each other again hit us both really hard. We didn't know what was going to happen next. All we knew was, something was going to happen. One of our early dates was very prophetic. In the early '80s, there was a club called Summerfields, one of the hotel bars in the part of town they called "The Strip" in Bloomington. For a big portion of the '70s, The Strip was a very popular destination for club-goers. Lots of bands, big singles bars, it was a popular place to see and be seen. By the early '80s, this popular gathering area was on its way down. It still had some life in it and Summerfields was one of the clubs still hanging on. Kristi had told me there was a band called The Spirit of St. Louis that was playing at Summerfields the entire week. When she lived in St. Louis for a couple of years, she had seen the band and gotten to know its manager and some of the band members. She suggested we should check them out. So on a ridiculously frigid night, we went to Summerfields to see the band.

Inside Summerfields, the band was doing a really good job of entertaining people. The band was tight. The singer-guitarist had a bit of Joe Cocker in him. Honestly, he was singing and playing his ass off. I was impressed. As good as the band was it really didn't matter; they were insignificant at that time to both of us. We were both focusing on each other and digging the fact that we were together. As we said goodbye to the band and went out to my car, I realized I left my keys in the car. Luckily for me I didn't lock my door. What wasn't so lucky was, I couldn't find my keys. They weren't on the floor, on the seat, under the seat, outside of the car, on the dash, you name it. I couldn't find them.

One thing that people close to me know is that I can handle almost anything except doing something incredibly stupid like losing my keys. It's my weakness, my Achilles heel. When I

Are you with the band?

lose my keys, it doesn't take me long to lose it. If I would have been alone in that freezing parking lot I would have been screaming obscenities for the world to hear, but I wasn't alone. Kristi was standing right next to me, freezing. I was embarrassed, humiliated, and angry—not a good combination for a new girlfriend to see, especially someone as special as Kristi was to me. After about twenty minutes of trying to find these keys, my feet hurt from being so cold and I was frustrated. Kristi suggested that we go inside the lobby and get warm.

When we got there she asked me to take my shoes off to get my feet warm. I gladly did that. Then she did something so selfless that it caught me off guard. She took my socks off and started rubbing my feet to get them warm. I think even while it was happening, I knew that the gesture Kristi did was significant. While I'm the last person to say a woman should do anything subservient to please a man, the fact that Kristi was so concerned about how cold I was and how frustrated I was to do something so selfless as to warm my feet and, in the process, calm me down, was something that really touched me. I know it was the kindest thing any girl had ever done for me. The act was small; the magnitude of that act was huge. It showed me that this was a woman who was concerned about my well-being. I also figured that if this were just another date for her, she would have never done something like touch another guy's cold feet. She wanted good things for me. I wanted nothing more than to make her happy. I wanted what was happening with us to continue.

One of the first things I did within the first couple of weeks that Kristi and I were going out was to call two girls I had been seeing occasionally. One was a girl in Janesville, Wisconsin. This relationship displayed all the highs and lows of a long distance relationship. We had a lot of fun together, but not seeing each other for months was getting old by the time I was seeing Kristi. We had basically stopped seeing each other, but it was still a relationship that was lingering. The other girl was someone I was working with at a restaurant. She was great, and we had a great time together. We were seeing each other more than my relationship with the Wisconsin girl, but it wasn't a serious thing. The bottom line was, I didn't want anything to interrupt what was happening with Kristi and me. One night, I called both of them and told them what was happening. I told them I started seeing somebody, a friend I'd known for a long time.

I told them that this new relationship was big for me and I needed to make clear that any chance of a relationship with either one of the girls was not going to happen. Now, it's quite possible each girl had already made that decision on their own before my call, but if they had, they hadn't told me yet. It seemed to me that both relationships were still possibilities. I didn't want those possibilities anymore. I suppose I could have tried going out with Kristi and the other two girls at the same time, but why? I knew I wanted to be with Kristi, and I had to clear the slate. This was big and I knew it.

As my relationship with Kristi became stronger, the only time we were separated was when I was at work or sleeping. We were falling deeply in love, and it was happening quickly. After nearly a year of seeing each other, an opportunity presented itself for me to join a full-time band. One night Kristi received a call from her friends in St. Louis. It was a call from The Spirit of St. Louis. They knew I was a singer. They inquired about my interest in coming to St. Louis to audition for their band as a lead singer. They wanted to stop being a "hotel band" and start the process of writing original material and playing freestanding clubs, as opposed to the hotel circuit. They'd done that same circuit for years, quite successfully, but they wanted a change. The opportunity in front of me was intimidating. I'd never performed in a full-time band that played five to six nights a week.

I didn't know if my voice could stand the strain. I'd always lived in Minneapolis, so for me to pack up everything and move to St. Louis to join a bunch of guys I didn't know was a big risk. The biggest risk was the possibility of Kristi and me being apart from each other. The timing was tough on both of us. Again, Kristi displayed her compassion and concern for my well-being. She encouraged me to drive down and audition. That's what we did. At the Viking Hotel in a suburb of St. Louis, I auditioned for the band. I felt I'd done a good job and my conversations with the bandleader went well. It seemed to me the job was mine to have if I wanted it. I did want it, but I didn't want to be in another long-distance relationship, especially with Kristi. In the hotel room after the audition, Kristi and I had a long talk about how we would deal with me living in St. Louis. She had moved home from St. Louis less than year before, so the fact that now I was moving to St. Louis, joining the band that she suggested we see on one of our first dates, was a bit surreal. As hard as it was going to be, we both agreed that it was a good challenge for me to do this. Less than a month later, I packed up all my earthly goods in my cramped and rickety black, Triumph TR7, drove twelve hours with my knees resting on my chin back to the Viking Hotel in St. Louis, and began my life away from Kristi, with a new band full of members I barely knew.

After a few months of long phone calls, love and lust letters to each other, and being lonely for each other, Kristi decided to pack up her things and move back to St. Louis so we could be together. It was great to have her with me. The separation we experienced for a few months did nothing to diminish what we felt for each other. It grew more intense now that we both lived in St. Louis. When I would come home from a week or two weeks away on the road, seeing Kristi in her car waiting for me to get out of the drummer's black van was fantastic. I still took a lot of pleasure that Kristi Knutson was digging me, the same me that put her on the Top Ten list all those years ago.

The earmarks of our early days together have proven to be a consistent theme throughout our twenty-year history of being together. It displays itself in the most obvious ways: The fact that, despite my weird job as a performer, we'll be celebrating our eighteenth wedding anniversary in April. The way our children carry themselves in public, how they treat their friends, the respect they have for us and the innate expectation to immediately be liked when they walk into a room, is a direct result of how we treat each other.

Kristi wants me to express my creativity because she understands that if she tried to muzzle that creativity it would alter the kind of man I am. She understands that I want to use my creativity to strengthen our family, both financially and morally. Being the wife of a musician is not easy. Maintaining any relationship is a tough road. Adding all the uncertainties and craziness of being the wife of someone performing live is potentially full of potholes. Despite that, it's a road that she has graciously traveled and one that she's encouraged and challenged me to travel. Any musician who has that kind of support stands a far better chance of reaching their goals musically and professionally. Being with someone who wants you to maintain that musical part of your life and not muzzle it because it isn't bringing in enough money is a blessing. I've been blessed.

Even when things were tough, the gigs were few and far between and the music I was playing was less than inspiring, Kristi was on my side. Without that support, doing what I do would be a lot tougher. I wouldn't be the man I am today. I wouldn't be the performer I am today. Actually, my career in this town as it stands now would have never happened. She gets me. She is and always will be, "with the band." I can't ask for more than that.

Heart & Soul became such a huge part of my life in 1994. Since then, it has given me direction and passion. I love the logo that Jim Taugher created. It's powerful. Heart & Soul has provided some inspiring musical moments in the Twin Cities. I miss it. It's coming back.

We give and give

S *ome musicians are perceived as egotistical and selfish.* Those two attributes are definitely in all musicians in one form or the other. If there's not a piece of you that's selfish or egotistical, you probably wouldn't have chosen to be a musician in the first place. You need those qualities to serve as your catalyst to get your music out there in the first place. If you didn't have some ego and selfishness, you'd never be able to handle the rejection of losing a gig, someone hating your song, not getting a record deal, and a thousand other rejections musicians face during their career. The balance you have to handle is how much of these attributes do you want the public and other musicians you play with to see? How you display these attributes to others is what makes each musician unique.

One of the most frustrating traits that a lot of musicians have that's linked to ego and selfishness is thinking that they're invincible personally and professionally. Maybe it's because the main focus of a musician's life is the pursuit of creativity and to further his or her career. Maybe it's because some think that there will always be someone there to pick up the pieces if something happens. The mundane matters of taking care of yourself personally and professionally are low on the list of priorities.

It's not as simple as to accuse some musicians of being naive, ignorant, or even stupid about it. Complacency plays a role. It's not very glamorous to think about setting money aside, or getting insurance to protect yourself if something happens to you. But like most unpleasant things, you can only avoid them for so long before they show up to slap you around at the most unexpected and vulnerable moments. Most of the time, not taking care of the important matters of the nonmusical aspects of a musician's life can be traced to a financial issue. The price you pay for not taking care of your own business can often be steep.

For as long as I've been a recognizable presence in the Twin Cities music scene, the call to action for musicians to help other musicians in need has been constant. Benefits are thrown for all sorts of ailments, illnesses, life-threatening diseases, stolen gear on the road, and others, all to help other musicians dig themselves out of the hole they found themselves in. It's a real tribute to the musical community that there are so many that choose to help others.

The positive aspects of this are obvious. Musicians are sharing their talent to help others. We should be doing that. We have a gift that the vast majority of people could never dream of having, even on a local level. The gift that we all worked so hard for comes with responsibility. One of the responsibilities is to do what you can, when you can, to help others. I've seen that firsthand as a recipient of a musician's generosity. I've given time myself to help others in need, and I was happy to do it. However, the longer I perform, it becomes more evident to me that it's important to involve myself in things that reach some kind of common sense resolution. What will the end result of my involvement be? Will the money raised be used wisely and used for what all of us volunteered for in the first place? It has to be about more than just a bunch of musicians getting together and jamming.

The actual act of donating your talent to help others can fall into different categories. The easiest way to tug at heartstrings is children. Children who are sick, suffering from a disease, suffering from a car accident, children who lost their parents, parents who lost their child to a car accident or a shooting, etc. These types of charitable events are hard to resist. If you're asked to do it because your name is recognizable enough in town, a serious effort should be made to help if you can. Of course, all requests for benefits can't be done, but as any caring human being, you want to help if you can. The decision to accept the offer is helped along if you're involvement will gain some notoriety or exposure to help your own career. That's not a bad thing, it's just reality. I counted on both the compassion and career savvy of local and national musicians when I began a very important phase of my life, using my talent and name in town to help others in need.

When it was obvious that my band, Mick Sterling and the Stud Brothers, was becoming a hot commodity doing our every Sunday night at Bunkers Music Bar and Grill in Minneapolis, I felt strongly that it was time to use this success to give back a bit. My daughter, Mikaela, was born, and we were expecting my son, Tucker, at any time. While I sure wasn't rich, I was in a good place professionally and couldn't have asked for more personally. I'm sure that motivated me to try something.

The first charitable thing I attempted at Bunkers was to help the homeless by having my audience donate food when they came into the bar. We attempted that for a while. It was relatively successful, but very disorganized, too many loose ends. While it didn't exactly turn out how I thought it would, it was a start. The next one I attempted required more planning, compromise, and dealing with more bands than just my band. I had an idea to help an organization called the St. Joseph's Home for Children, based in Minneapolis. This is a place where kids can go if they find themselves in trouble, or if their parents are going through something that requires their kids to be away from them for a while to resolve things. The woman who was my contact, Connie Skillingstad, was terrific. She asked me to see if I could do something to help. I wanted to give it a shot. The concept was to find multiple local bands and do a benefit concert. I chose the Guthrie Theater in Minneapolis to do the show. I talked to the woman who was booking the Guthrie back then and also to promoter Sue McLean, now of Sue McLean and Associates. I was a novice at doing something like this so I needed advice from a lot of folks at the Guthrie to make it work. There was the cost of the actual venue, the sound system, insurance, scheduling, finding the bands, and a hundred other things to deal with. I was eager and a bit terrified. Despite that, it was onward and upward. I was able to get a wide array of top talent to do this show. All of the groups donated their show. I had the reggae group The Maroons, Twin Cities songwriter Paul Metsa, a solo perform-ance by one of the most soulful singers I'd ever heard at the time, Mark Lickteig, the Excelsior Gospel Choir, three of the top female singers in town, Gwen Matthews, Debbie Duncan, and Cynthia Johnson, and my own band. The plan was simple. Whatever proceeds raised through tickets, would go directly to the St. Joseph's Home for Children.

I had the concept. The bands confirmed. I started promot-ing it with the tools I had at my disposal. There was just one problem: no one was buying tickets. Not only that, I was a long way from even covering the expenses of the room. I didn't have a Plan B. It was time to make one up.

I decided that I would chip away at ticket sales by calling all the local restaurants in Minneapolis to see if they'd buy ten tickets, valued at a total of $100 for their employees. It required a lot of time on the phone trying reach each manager and making my pitch. One thing that did surprise me was how many people had actually heard of my band or me. That helped a lot. It got me in the door and afforded me a couple more minutes to make my pitch. Because of all the phone calls and visiting the restaurants, I was able to raise enough ticket revenue to at least come close to paying the venue. Now all that remained was to see how many people showed up at the Guthrie on the event night.

One cool thing about the event was the fact that my band was going to be playing on the world famous Guthrie stage. The stage where Led Zeppelin, Elton John, Springsteen, and countless other legends made their Twin Cities debut. It was the best place in town to play. I should have been intimidated about that, but I was too busy worrying about other things to focus on what a big deal this was for me. I wasn't sure if the other groups had played the stage before. All I knew was that I hadn't. When you're in the thick of producing an event, you have a tendency to lose track of how special it actually is. Such is the curse of an organizer.

As the doors of the Guthrie Theater opened that night, it was quickly apparent that the amount of tickets I'd sold to restaurants was not translating to people in the seats. We also had very little walk-up audience. That combination meant it was going to be a slow night at the Guthrie. Very disappointing, but the show must go on.

As the first act began, I looked out and there may have been two hundred people in the audience. That was a lot of empty seats to look at. It didn't improve as the show went on. As a matter of fact, the crowd grew smaller. The show was going on far too long, I desperately needed a stage manager to tell people to limit their sets so everyone could get on stage on time. As my band played the last set, there may have been fifty people in the audience. Lots of thoughts were racing in my mind while I was performing. As a performer, I should have been upset that so few people were in the crowd to see my first show at the Guthrie. Fortunately, my producer hat took over to hide that pain for later.

My biggest concern was how little money, if any, I was going to be able to send to St. Joseph's. As the night drew to a close, I found myself with a healthy dose of self-pity and looking for any outlet to blame. In the end, it came down to me being a novice. I did some things right. Mostly I did a lot of things without thinking it through. Fortunately for me, the Guthrie took mercy on me and reduced many of their theatre costs because they saw what happened. Because of that, I was able to send around $3,000 from ticket sales and private donations to St. Joseph's from that night. Not nearly the amount I wanted to send but, again, it was a start.

A couple of years later, a woman came into my life that changed my professional and personal life. Little did I know that the message this woman had would define my professional life for years to come. As with a lot of huge moments in my life, it happened at Bunkers, and Kristi was the reason I found out about it.

Our Sunday nights at Bunkers were consistently filled with lines out the door. On nights when it preceded a holiday on Monday, they were even bigger. I didn't require a lot of perks. But one of the things I did request was having one table, or even one chair, reserved for my wife Kristi. It was on this night, the night before Labor Day in 1994, that a woman came up to Kristi and introduced herself as the director of development for a place called Camp Heartland. As the band was playing, the director, Susan Keating, told Kristi about Camp Heartland. After the first set, Kristi told me about Susan and said we should speak. We actually did speak a bit at the table, but it was so loud and hectic in the club, that I could only hear about every other word she was saying. Somehow through the noise, we made arrangements to speak over the phone after Labor Day. That Tuesday, I called Susan. What Susan told me affected me deeply. Susan told me the mission of Camp Heartland. The official description in 1994 was that they were helping children either afflicted or affected by HIV/AIDS attend summer camp. But what she was telling went far deeper than that.

Back in 1994, confusion, misinformation, and sometimes outright hysteria about AIDS was commonplace. It was not too long after Magic Johnson announced he had the HIV virus. Ryan White, who gained such notoriety for his courage and his outlook about having AIDS, had just passed away. Living with HIV/AIDS back in the early '90s meant you were not only living in fear of a fatal illness, but also dealing with a scarlet letter scenario from the public. People were afraid.

For some, they showed their fear in very hurtful ways. As an adult living with HIV in the early '90s, it must have been mentally and physically exhausting. As a child living with HIV during the same time period, throw in the fact that you've barely started your life and there was a very real possibility you wouldn't live past your twentieth birthday. That's some heavy lifting for a kid.

It's tough enough being a kid with all the things life throws at you, let alone having the kids in school being afraid that you may infect them with a deadly disease. That's what the kids who attended Camp Heartland were dealing with. Some of them were afraid to go public with their disease. Imagine trying to keep that secret. Camp Heartland provided these kids with an all-expenses-paid week of summer camp with a bunch of kids who were going through the same thing. A chance for these kids to share what they're feeling with other kids going through the same thing. No parents. Just a real summer camp, with a full medical staff at all times. This made sense to me.

A young man named Neil Willenson founded Camp Heartland. Neil had heard about a kid in his hometown in Wisconsin who was living with HIV/AIDS. The town was afraid. This child was not allowed to go to regular summer camps because of his illness. Neil got some college friends together and started raising money. Through their efforts, they were able to fund the first Camp Heartland session in Wisconsin. Very inspiring stuff.

During our phone conversation, Susan mentioned that CBS was doing a feature-documentary film called *Angelie's Secret*. The film was focusing on a young girl named Angelie, who was living with HIV/AIDS. A considerable amount of time in the film was going to be focused on Angelie's visit to Camp Heartland. It also focused on what role Camp Heartland played in her decision to go public and how the support she received at the camp eased her uneasiness about it and gave her some confidence in what she was about to do. The film was being narrated by Julia Roberts. Camp Heartland was eager for the film to raise awareness about what they were trying to do—help a lot of kids going through the same thing and raise a lot of money so they could send more kids to Camp Heartland.

Susan had asked me to see if I had some interest in doing a benefit show for Camp Heartland on one of my Sundays at Bunkers. My response was that I would be happy to do it, but I didn't think it would raise much revenue.

Sometimes when so many people are in one room, it's hard to get their attention to make a donation. Plus, Camp Heartland was relatively unknown in the Minneapolis area, so that would make it tough. Mostly, I just didn't think it would raise much money, at least not enough to make an impact. My thought was that it would be great to capitalize on the timing of the documentary by producing a show at the Guthrie, Northrop Auditorium, or the State Theater in Minneapolis prior to the airing of the film on CBS. After I hung up the phone and discussed it with Kristi, I decided to take that plan of action and see what could develop.

As I started making phone inquiries about venue availability and costs, it was clear that there was nothing available during the timeframe I wanted. It was time to regroup and come up with another plan.

My new plan was to contact various clubs in the Twin Cities area and do a week-long series of shows featuring local bands, all to raise money for one charity, Camp Heartland. At the time, I didn't remember anybody else doing something like this, so it seemed like this concept would stand out. My goal was to include clubs like the Fine Line, The Cabooze, Bunkers, First Avenue, as well as trying to do something at the now defunct Planet Hollywood in the Mall of America. The other goal was to make the lineup as musically diverse as I could think of to reflect the diversity of kids who were living with HIV/AIDS. The plan was as set as anything can be when you're making it up as you go. It was a crazy idea, but I was determined to get this done.

The phone calls were fast and furious in my north Minneapolis home the next few months. The first thing I needed to do was to find some financial sponsorship. I was fortunate enough to find some support from a person who had invested in one my early CDs. I went to his office and told him what I wanted to do for Camp Heartland. Thankfully, he provided seed money to take care of the expenses to make this happen. The next step was to find some way to promote this event.

I cold-called WCCO-TV and was connected with Kiki Rosatti. We'd never met before. I think she may have seen my band at Bunkers. For some reason unknown to me, she actually agreed to meet with me at her office. I was just a guy off the street with an idea. At that time, I don't remember WCCO-TV ever sponsoring any type of musical event, let alone one that lasted seven days for one charity. All I knew was that I had a great story to tell and I was passionate about making it happen. Thankfully, Kiki saw that at our meeting. In a few days, I got the word that WCCO-TV was in my corner. They would provide some PSA spots and promote the event. That was huge to me. It meant that this idea had some credibility in the business world. It meant that people were going to find out about it.

The next step was to find the bands, tell them the story, and ask them to donate their show. To their credit, nearly all the bands jumped right in. They heard what it was about and they were happy to do it. I had nothing to guarantee them as far as exposure. The only thing I could guarantee them was that since this was a multiple band lineup at each club, they'd stand a good chance of playing for a new audience instead of their own fans. It was heartwarming to me that the bands appreciated what I was trying to do.

The first year of Heart & Soul was filled with amazing bands. The lineup included Babes in Toyland, House of Large Sizes, the Honeydogs, Molly and the Heymakers, and G. B. Leighton at First Avenue; the Spanic Boys at Bunkers; the Curbfeelers and Tribe of Millions at the Fine Line; and many other bands and other clubs. To kick off the week of music, we did a Sunday gospel brunch at Planet Hollywood. This day was filled with the wonderful voices of Gwen Matthews, Debbie Duncan, and Jenny Sanford, as well as an acoustic show with some of the members of my band.

As the Sunday brunch drew to a close, I introduced Neil Willenson, the founder of Camp Heartland. Some of the kids who attended Camp Heartland said a few words of thanks to everyone attending and explained how it felt to go to Camp Heartland. I said a few words myself. Everyone in the room that day knew that Camp Heartland was a very, very special thing. It was an emotional and uplifting day. There were lots of tears on that Sunday, including mine. Good work was being done.

It was a great way to start the week of music. By the end of the week, we were able to send nearly $19,000 from ticket sales, cover charges, and donations to Camp Heartland. That wasn't bad considering the average cover was $6 per show.

Luck played a huge part in our first year. For our First Avenue show, the generosity and kind advice from the face of First Avenue, Steve McClellan, provided Heart & Soul with a profit that it shouldn't have had. While our show was successful that night, we were not able to cover all the club expenses and send a donation. Steve showed mercy on the event and donated some of the club expenses so we could be profitable for the evening. It was a lot of work for my wife, select members of Camp Heartland, our public relations person at the time, Dale Ann Murphy, and me, but well worth it. Heart & Soul made a statement that week. Not the most organized statement, but a solid and emotional statement nonetheless.

The momentum Heart & Soul experienced in the first year made me want to expand the event in the second year. One huge thing that happened in the second year was the phenomenon of a young man named Jonny Lang.

It's safe to say that without the involvement of Jonny Lang, the success of Heart & Soul that year, and the following years, would not have been possible. The timing was perfect for Heart & Soul for someone like Jonny to come along. The success of Jonny Lang in the Twin Cities at that time was truly remarkable, considering that it wasn't even a year prior that Jonny did one of his first shows playing in front of my band at an outdoor festival in Fargo. At that time, he was actually playing the sax and a small amount of rhythm guitar. He seemed very shy on stage, but I do remember not taking my eyes of him. The easiest hook was of course how young he was, but there was obviously something else. Six months later, Jonny was playing in front of my band again at an outdoor tent party in Anoka. When I walked in the tent, I saw a sea of bodies right in front of the stage and this young man singing and playing his ass off, energizing the crowd better than any local artist I knew about. When he finished, the line to buy his merchandise was unlike anything I'd ever seen from a local performer. This was special. Following Jonny that night was not one of my favorite moments performing. I got my butt kicked and my butt wasn't even in the room yet. That night told me that I had to find a way to get Jonny to do Heart & Soul. It was a perfect fit. He was a teenager. Camp Heartland helped kids. The timing was perfect.

I wanted to keep the basic concept of Heart & Soul the same, but I was eager to send more money to Camp Heartland. I needed to have one of the nights for Heart & Soul be viewed as the signature night. A night that would feature higher visibility bands, higher ticket prices, auction items and more. All the stuff that real benefits attempt to do. Since I had no idea how to do that, I figured I had better ask someone who knew how to do these shows. The best person I could see doing it was Dino Lopesio.

Dino was the event coordinator for many of the most popular events at one of the premiere event centers in Minneapolis, International Market Square. He had produced events for the top rock and pop station in the Twin Cities, KDWB, for many years. These events featured live music, a huge stage, food, raffles, and much more. Thousands of people attended these events. His events were hot tickets. I wanted to get Heart & Soul in that league. I met with Dino to ask his advice to help me get there.

One pleasant surprise when I met with Dino was how open and giving he was with good advice for me. I'm sure he must have thought I was a bit naïve attempting something like this, but he liked my concept. Dino was knowledgeable about what was going on. He latched onto my concept about getting Jonny involved in Heart & Soul. He thought if I could get Jonny locked in, doing a show at International Market Square could work. I had no money to pay Dino for his services. Despite that, Dino became a great mentor for me. He became my advisor on all the details within International Market Square. He had worked with them so often he could tell me what to ask for, production items that were needed for the venue, and many other things. He encouraged me and he also reigned me in when I was trying to do too much. Eventually, a plan was agreed on for the second year.

The content for the main portion of the event was to remain the same: multiple clubs, multiple bands, and a diverse musical lineup. The plan for the signature event was going to feature Jonny Lang, the great reggae band Ipso Facto, and Mick Sterling and the Stud Brothers. The event was growing. In order for it to work, the event needed more financial sponsorship. What followed proved to me that something about this event was blessed and meant to happen.

I was doing an afternoon outdoor event at a new Lifetime Fitness location in Woodbury, Minnesota. I was one of the singers for a throw-together band that was performing at Lifetime's grand opening celebration. During the event, I ran into one of the personal trainers at Lifetime, Dan Kelly, who had seen my band at Bunkers. Dan had heard about Heart & Soul the year before and was interested in what was going to happen the following year. I told him some of the plans and shared with him that in order for that to happen, we needed some financial sponsorship. He suggested that a meeting be set with the founder of Lifetime Fitness, Bahram Akradi. In a few days, that meeting happened. Our lunch meeting was at Kincaids in Bloomington, Minnesota. Susan Keating from

Camp Heartland and I met Bahram. While we waited to order, I filled Bahram in about what happened with Heart & Soul last year and the plans for this year. Susan filled him in on what Camp Heartland was all about. Another thing that helped was that Dino and Bahram were friends. In a span of twenty minutes, Bahram had agreed in principle to provide Heart & Soul with a financial donation doubling what I received last year. What made it even better was that payback was not required. It was a true financial sponsorship. It was thrilling. It provided Heart & Soul with enough money to make it happen.

Now that we had the financial sponsorship, it was time to finalize all the bands and get the word out about what was going to happen. My relationship with WCCO-TV had continued for our second year. I made arrangements with Jonny Lang's management, the Twin-Cities-based Blue Sky Artist Management, to confirm his participation. One of the things I wanted to happen with Jonny's involvement was that Jonny be available for some radio interviews to promote the show. I wanted him to hear about what Camp Heartland did prior to doing the show. These interviews proved have a lasting effect on his involvement for many years. When it was agreed to have Jonny involved in our second year, I'm confident he found out from his agent and management and they told him it was just another gig. I don't think he really understood what the scope of Heart & Soul was really about. As his dad and Jonny would meet me at radio stations, he started finding out.

Jonny was very hot in town, and he was getting the same questions about his age. The main thrust of the questions were inquiries about how could he play and sing the blues at such a young age, so on and so on. Heart & Soul was different and I think he was starting to realize it. As we did more interviews, he felt more comfortable talking about his involvement in this charitable event. Prior to the event, he showed up at a photo shoot for our

WCCO ads and he really connected with the kids. He was their age. He was one of them. He was helping them.

Powerful stuff was happening and it was a thrill for me to be around it. Even with the help of members of Camp Heartland and Dino Lopesio, my wife, along with a few select friends, and I did the main grunt work of Heart & Soul. This was truly a grassroots operation. One of the things Dino suggested was that we send out flyers to select mailing lists announcing the event. This meant addressing, stuffing, and stamping five thousand to six thousand envelopes. Trying to find people help you stuff that many envelopes is like asking people to help you move. They begrudgingly do it, and they can't wait to be done. We cleared the furniture from our living room, made room on the floor, sat in a circle, and started stuffing, writing, licking, and sorting, in that order. Seven hours later, after starting with eight to ten people, Kristi and I were sitting on our bed, zombie-eyed with no surviving taste buds from licking so many stamps. Kristi and I got it done. If there are any women out there under the impression that sharing the same bed with me would be a thrill, I can safely say that I have my moments, but there were no moments that night. That's what they mean when they say for better or for worse when you're married. After I woke up from my zombie state of mind, I mailed all the letters the next day. It didn't take long to find out the response.

From our ads in the Twin Cities weekly newspaper *City Pages,* the flyers, the ads on WCCO-TV, and the stature of Jonny Lang in the Twin Cities, the response to attend our International Market Square (IMS) event was intense. People called my home phone. I took their orders over the phone. I mailed out all the tickets. I answered all the questions from people. I reserved all the tables for people who were eating dinner as well as attending the concert. I made the bank deposits. I made copies of the checks. I met with Dino and the staff of Atrium Catering at IMS to go over the final details. Although I

We give and give

was receiving help from Camp Heartland and Kristi, the vast majority of the things concerning the event and the venue were basically in my head. I didn't think too much about it at the time. I did at six-thirty on the night of the event.

The morning and afternoon of the IMS show were filled with tons of final details to be taken care of. Our production coordinator, Micha McFarlane, covered lots of production items. Dino was on-site for some of the day to deal with the staff at IMS and other production aspects. I was still getting calls for tickets so I was checking my home voicemail a lot during that day getting will call tickets arranged. We had already had a huge week's worth of shows in various clubs that raised a respectable amount of money. Heart & Soul was very fortunate to have the participation of another leading band in the Twin Cities, G. B. Leighton, to serve as one of our main draws for the week. I was energized, but I was tired too. Eventually all the pieces—the stage, bands, food, tables, valet, coat checks, insurance, sound, lights, techs, banners, artist catering, towels, stage times, tickets, and ticket takers—seemed to fall in line. That's what I thought until I walked down to the IMS lobby.

At six-thirty as I looked at the lobby, I felt a strange combination of joy and fear. Joy because unlike my benefit show at the Guthrie a couple of years before, I was looking at a lobby full of around five hundred people waiting to get into the show. They were pumped. The valets were scrambling. It was going to be a big show. Fear because as I looked at the eager crowd, I realized something. I didn't tell anybody anything about the venue itself. I had barely any volunteers to escort people to their tables that were located on multiple levels. Nobody from Camp Heartland, or even my wife had ever been to IMS before that night. They had no idea how to assist me. I had no help. It wasn't because people didn't offer to help, I just didn't delegate any authority. I didn't tell anybody anything about the night itself. I was hosting a party of four thousand people, and I was basically the only one who knew how the night was going to go. I tried to remain calm, but inside I was absolutely freaking out and upset with myself for being so stupid.

Somehow through the madness, people I considered angels to me that night stepped up and tried to decipher my ramblings as they helped me get people to their seats. I was running around the event center trying to keep things together. I don't know how well I did, but despite my best efforts to screw things up, the show did go on.

I was never so happy to be on stage playing with my band then I was that night. Performing was my form of escape from the chaos I created by keeping all the information about the event in my head. By the time my band hit the stage as the first act, the crowd was huge. Five levels of people were looking over the balcony, and the floor was full of people shoved up against the stage. The room was electric. All of these people were finding out about Camp Heartland through information at the door and seeing some of the kids who attended Camp Heartland on our stage. It was like our Planet Hollywood show multiplied by three hundred. Through all the self-inflicted chaos, somehow we pulled this off.

As the night came to a close and the crew was tearing the stage down and the IMS staff was cleaning up the place for another event the following night, I found myself walking around the space with Jonny. His show, as expected, electrified the crowd and he tore the roof off the place. As we walked, we talked about his show that night. He thought he had a good show, but he was always having good shows back then. I told him that this was more than just a show. He had no idea at the time how much good he had actually done just sharing his talent with people. Maybe someone his age couldn't be expected to understand the magnitude of something like this, but I sure did. He was special, and Heart & Soul was very fortunate to get him. His contribution that night became a yearly commitment for Jonny for the next five years to help Heart & Soul help Camp Heartland. That night proved to me that it only takes a good idea, good advice, and a few compassionate people to achieve something great.

For the next few years, Heart & Soul grew in stature and in scope. In our fourth year, we decided to move our main event into the parking lot at Bunkers Music Bar and Grill. We put two large stages under a big tent that covered the parking lot. Our lineup featured Jonny Lang, Shannon Curfman, a great Native American rock and blues group, Indigenous, another great friend to Heart & Soul, G. B. Leighton, Renee Austin, and many others. One act that we tried to fit in that weekend but couldn't make it work, was the legendary bluesman, Luther Allison. The involvement of Luther Allison defined the spirit of Heart & Soul in a way only Luther could do.

The Metropolitan Event Center in Golden Valley was the site for our Heart & Soul night featuring Luther Allison. At the time, Luther was being managed by Miki Mulvehill (Miki Nord now) of Blue Sky Artist Management. Miki was one of the early supporters of Heart & Soul, so she pushed very hard to make sure that Luther could do this show. Luther and his band, featuring one of the top guitar players in the Midwest in James Solberg, arrived at the Metropolitan club that day after a twelve-hour trip.

The live performances of Luther Allison were infamous for their length and intensity. He was truly a legend, and I was very proud to have him involved in Heart & Soul. With a lot of the artists performing at Heart & Soul, I would watch them a bit, but then move on and concentrate on keeping the event on track. With Luther, that practice went right out the window. One thing about Luther was that, when he was on stage, he demanded your attention. He got mine. His performance and his commitment to his audience riveted me. He was magnetic and mesmerizing. As he walked through the crowd, ripping off a ten-minute fiery guitar solo, the crowd was smiling and touching him. Luther, probably dead tired after his long trip, worked the crowd like a champ. From the minute Luther hit the stage, the fans were on their feet, screaming. He owned the crowd. I'd never seen anything quite like it. Even James Brown at The Cabooze didn't receive that kind of devotion from his crowd. It was inspiring. Luther was the real thing.

After the show, Luther talked to a bunch of his fans that were waiting for him in front of the stage. He met my kids and some of the kids from Camp Heartland who were at the show. He couldn't have been more gracious and friendly with everyone he met. Even though he had been in the room for hours, I still hadn't actually met him. Sometime during post performance, Miki came up to me and said that Luther had decided to not accept the performance fee for the night. He decided to donate his show. I was stunned. I walked up to Luther and introduced myself. He then confirmed what Miki told me. I couldn't believe it. This was a man who drove more than twelve hours to do this show. A show that he was receiving far less than his normal performance fee as it was. The magnitude of this man was evident to me while he was performing. This incredible gesture on his part confirmed to me that this was a giant of a man. I'll never forget it.

What we came to find out later that same summer was that the Heart & Soul show would be the second-to-last show Luther Allison would ever perform in the Twin Cities. Luther was diagnosed with cancer that summer. He passed away a few weeks after finding out. It was a huge loss in the blues world— a huge loss for the music world in general. It hit all of the people connected with Heart & Soul hard. Luther blessed us. In honor of Luther, Miki and I recommended that, every year, the main stage for Heart & Soul be named The Luther Allison Memorial Stage. It was a fitting tribute to the man who left his ego, played the music, and loved the people.

The following years of Heart & Soul were filled with fantastic musical performances from artists like Martin Sexton, Tony Lucca, Mary Cutrufello, Michelle Branch, Monte Montgomery, Anders Osborne, Storyville, Kenny Wayne Shepherd, Delbert McClinton, Double Trouble, Syl Johnson, and Susan Tedeschi, as well as our annual performances from G. B. Leighton, Mick Sterling and the Stud Brothers, and Jonny Lang. It was important for me to maintain musical integrity. I think we achieved that.

The following years also provided many examples of growing pains as the event grew larger in scope. There were more volunteers, a board of directors, more production items, flights, hotels, rental cars, more merchandise, and other expense items. As an event gets larger, the amount of control you have with something you create begins to dwindle. You have to delegate and let things go. In many ways, that's a great thing. In some ways, there are headaches involved.

There are so many things that seem important when you produce an event like Heart & Soul. The biggest obstacle and challenge you have to face is finding the appropriate amount of financial sponsorship to get expenses paid. I was very fortunate with Heart & Soul that a lot of the production vendors would provide a reduced rate for their services because it was a charity. Once we decided to take the show outside, all of the artists donated. However, if it were a national band, we would pay for airfare, hotel, and ground transportation to get them to and from the show. Nearly five hundred volunteers worked the event. The board of directors took care of the administrative needs of the event. As the founder and event manager, this event was taking up hundreds of hours of my time. Because of that, I arranged with Camp Heartland and the board of directors of Heart & Soul to receive a small salary for my services throughout the year. There seemed to be countless meetings with volunteers, board members, mini sessions, sponsors, radio station representatives, salespeople, and other vendors. This little idea of mine had progressed like I imagined it. However, each year the event grew, the more concern there was with certain people within the recipient of our events, Camp Heartland.

Each year we did the event for Camp Heartland, we made a profit. Although there were certain members from Camp Heartland who spent a large amount of time and energy on Heart & Soul, at no time did Camp Heartland ever risk any cash to produce Heart & Soul. At the insistence of Camp Heartland after our third year, it was decided that Heart & Soul become its own 501c3 nonprofit organization to reduce risk for both parties. Camp Heartland chose particular members to be on the new board of directors for Heart & Soul. The objective and goal was twofold; do everything possible to raise as much money for Camp Heartland as we could through Heart & Soul events and make sure that Camp Heartland was never at risk in case something went wrong. The completion of a separate 501c3 paperwork for Heart & Soul was the safeguard.

Another safeguard the Heart & Soul board begrudgingly took was to get rain insurance. This was a costly proposition, but one I thought was well overdue. Each year we did the event, it was a beautiful sunny day in the '80s. It would only rain after the second show was done on Sunday night while the crew tore down the stage. It was just a matter of time.

On our Sunday show in 2001, it rained from nine in the morning and basically didn't stop until the following Friday afternoon. Heart & Soul was facing its first rainout. We had a brave crowd of a fifteen hundred to two thousand people who

We give and give

hung in there with us, waiting for it to stop raining. Fortunately for us, we had set up a huge tent in one the parking lots that was serving as our second stage. Because of the rain, we had to transfer all of our main stage artists to the tent stage. This was a huge ordeal because the stage was much smaller; we didn't have the gear or monitor mixes requested by the national artists. To make matters even dicier, all of the artists were donating their show. It was miserable outside. As all the cold and soaking wet techs, volunteers, and volunteers leaders scrambled about, there was one aspect of the event that was more important than all the other chaotic things surrounding. Through all the activity and split-second decisions that needed to be made, my mind was only on one thing: the little beaker that collected the rain in the middle of Bunkers parking lot, watched ever so closely by the Weather Observer we paid $250 a day to sit on a chair and stare at the beaker.

That little beaker was going to decide the fate of our event in 2001. That little beaker cost us thousands of dollars to get there. It was part of the rain insurance policy that Heart & Soul finally decided to get for our event. It was not an easy decision to make for the board of directors, but we finally made it.

It was a serious risk of thousands of dollars. If the event happened and it was sunny both days, we were out thousands of dollars. If it didn't surpass the one-half inch of rain between the hours of 2:00 and 7:00 P.M. on the Sunday of the event, we were out thousands of dollars, despite the fact that the rain would destroy our walk up audience. With that in mind, as miserable as it was outside, all I was doing was praying for it to rain harder and faster to meet our policy deadline.

Once again, despite the ugliness outside, the gods, and, as the queen of Heart & Soul Miki Nord said that day, Luther Allison was looking down on us. It rained more than one-half inch. Our policy kicked in. Because of it, Heart & Soul was able to send nearly $100,000 to Camp Heartland in 2001, despite dodging a bullet, the rain, and a huge reduction in our walk-up crowd. We survived the weekend, but the backlash of that weekend was soon to be felt.

When any organization gets bigger, the original vision is always altered to accommodate the new voices contributing to the concept. When that happens, there's always a good chance that tensions and second-guessing will arise. Unfortunately, this happened between Camp Heartland and Heart & Soul. The fact that it happened is in no way reflective of the kind of organization the camp is. They continue to do vital work.

The camp's founder, Neil Willenson, and his board of directors have influenced and educated thousands about HIV/AIDS. The reputation of Camp Heartland is fantastic. The camp counselors and volunteers are the best of the best. Most importantly, the kids who attend are grateful for the existence of Camp Heartland. But what was becoming clear after our 2001 event was that things were starting to get a bit ugly. Heart & Soul's growing pains were now moving in to serious personality conflicts. There were disagreements within the board and certain members of Camp Heartland who were on the Heart & Soul board. Board members had problems with particular volunteer leaders. Certain board members were expressing concern about how I accomplished things due in part to the fact that I was being paid a small monthly fee to do the multitude of duties I performed for Heart & Soul. The board of Camp Heartland, despite the nearly $100,000 donated in 2001 and the previous $200,000 along with all kinds of in-kind and promotional support we provided them since 1995, was continuing to focus on the risk factor of the event growing so large and their perceived loss of control of an event of which they were the benefactor.

The biggest immediate concern from the 2001 event was that if the rain insurance didn't kick in, Heart & Soul wouldn't have been able to pay all of our production costs. Camp Heartland was concerned that if there was any debt from a Heart & Soul event, that vendors would go after Camp Heartland to get paid. This concern was puzzling to me and other Heart & Soul board members simply due to the fact that Camp Heartland was never in financial risk from a Heart & Soul event. We had jointly, between the board of directors for Heart & Soul and the board of directors for Camp Heartland, set a business plan up to protect Camp Heartland in the event we ever found ourselves in debt, specifically maintaining to separate 501c3 organizations. All of the billing for the event was addressed to Heart & Soul, not Camp Heartland. Despite those assurances, issues still arose.

Another concern for the camp officials was that they were counting on a certain level of donation to fit into their year-round budget. The motivation for that was pure. They wanted to send as many kids to Camp Heartland as possible. Certain members of Camp Heartland spent a huge amount of time and energy focusing on Heart & Soul. The board of Camp Heartland was starting to focus on whether all the time spent could potentially be spent in a more time effective and financially effective manner. Camp Heartland, rightly or wrongly, would count on a certain amount of money to be raised each year. If we didn't reach that amount, it would affect the rest of their plans for the rest of the year. Because the event was so dependent on walk-up business, Heart & Soul couldn't predict a certain total to send them. It depended on many things. All Heart & Soul knew was that we were going to send them as much as we could. The combination of these matters, and growing personality clashes between their board and the Heart & Soul board finally came to a head.

This beautiful little event that I started in my living room at my house in north Minneapolis was getting ugly. It was as if all of us were still soaking wet from the event that happened three months before. We couldn't shake it. Things were evolving in a dramatic fashion. Ironically, the word of how Camp Heartland decided to separate itself from Heart & Soul came down a few months later on Labor Day weekend, nearly eight years to the day I found out about Camp Heartland at Bunkers.

I got the news on the Thursday before Labor Day that despite how grateful they were for all of the years of support from Heart & Soul, it was time for them to separate themselves from us. There were just too many disagreements within the board of Camp Heartland about the direction Heart & Soul was taking. It was getting too big. They perceived it was too much of a financial risk. They were also concerned about the request from the Heart & Soul board that members of Camp Heartland remove themselves from the Heart & Soul board. Heart & Soul's perspective was that having members of Camp Heartland on the Heart & Soul Board could be perceived as a conflict of interest. Camp Heartland's perspective was that if they weren't on the Heart & Soul board, they wouldn't retain enough control. I know this sounds a bit strange, but if you live in the nonprofit world for a while, it would make more sense. The combination of all those factors made them feel they didn't have enough control over an event that was dedicated to them.

It was a mess. It was a tough phone call for Neil Willenson to make to me. We'd been through a lot together. Although I didn't like what he was saying to me, I understood his position. We were both in the middle, trying to soothe heated emotions on our respective sides.

My reply to Neil was that if this was the final decision of his board, let's at least finish it properly. Let's do one more year together and tell people it's our last year. There was no reason to end this so abruptly. After all Heart & Soul had done for Camp Heartland, financially and promotionally, not to mention the unmistakable goodwill the event created toward Camp Heartland in the Twin Cities, I urged Neil to go back to his board of directors to ask for one more year. I thought we at least deserved that consideration. He agreed to check in with them one more time. Forty-five minutes later, Neil called me again and said the decision was still the same.

After eight years and hundreds of thousands of dollars donated, Camp Heartland would no longer be affiliated with Heart & Soul. I concluded after that conversation that Heart & Soul was finished. Despite Heart & Soul's lack of involvement with Camp Heartland today, our introduction of Camp Heartland to their former promotions person, Kris Noble of Cities 97, now a Clear Channel radio station in Minneapolis, has proven to be a continued asset to Camp Heartland. For many years, Cities 97 has included Camp Heartland as one of the charities who receive funds from its hugely successful "Cities Sampler" CDs. They also have produced an event called "Hope in the Heartland," featuring one of the national artists that Cities 97 plays on the station. The time commitment from Camp Heartland's perspective is far less, plus they have a giant corporation like Clear Channel to get things done much more easily because of their clout in the industry. The long-term relationship with Clear Channel and, specifically, Cities 97 was due in large part to Heart & Soul. Since the main reason for Heart & Soul was to send as many kids as possible to Camp Heartland, the sustained relationship with Camp Heartland and Cities 97 is something I take pride in. I regret that Heart & Soul is not a part of it anymore, but things change and you have to make the best of it when it does. This left us with was one question: What do we do now?

After consideration from all of our board members and close friends, it was decided that Heart & Soul had done too much to stop now. We would try and help some other children's charity with the tools we had at our disposal. We set a plan in motion to diversify and reach out to larger and multiple children's charities and attempt to raise as much money for them as we did for Camp Heartland. One of the main objectives was to find charities that already had a strong infrastructure to help us raise more awareness about the event and to sell tables to the black-tie-dinner portion of the event that we always held the night before the concert event. After consideration from our board and multiple meetings, we found three very worthy children's charities for our 2002 event.

I hate hindsight. It so rarely conjures up something positive. Hindsight shows up mainly when something went wrong, or hints or signals were missed or ignored. As we began our efforts to do our 2002 event, that old Mr. Hindsight was just on the perimeter, waiting for us to come look him up. As soon as we began our efforts for 2002, it was clear that it was going to be a tough road.

The fact that Camp Heartland was no longer involved with Heart & Soul was very confusing to existing and potential sponsors. I can understand that reaction because it was confusing to me at the time, and I was there. Heart & Soul was so tied in with Camp Heartland in the Twin Cities that the common perception was that they were the same charity. Even though we were helping three very worthy charities in 2002, it wasn't Camp Heartland. The charities we chose, while doing fantastic work, were very large in scope. They did a bunch of different things to help kids. The issue was they did so much it was hard to explain. It took a paragraph to explain each one. The beauty about Camp Heartland was that all you needed was one sentence. They send kids with HIV/AIDS to summer camp. Short and sweet. You can visualize that very easily.

It used to be very easy to promote Heart & Soul. Now, it was becoming an ordeal. Despite the difficulty of getting our message out, we were working fast and furious with our sponsors and with clients our radio sponsor brought on board. Our goals were the same as they'd been in the year before: a black tie dinner on Friday night, this time in a tent underneath the huge awning next to the new event center, The Depot in downtown Minneapolis. On Saturday, the Ride with Heart & Soul Motorcycle Rally would leave from St. Paul Harley-Davidson at ten in the morning. At the same time, our weekend concert event was in the final stages of being set up for a two o'clock gate opening. Unlike last year, the weather forecast called for sunny skies. What they also mentioned was that the temperature was going to be in the '40s and '50s. This proved to be a bigger problem than the rain.

Our black tie event had all the elements of a beautiful gala: fantastic food, great silent auction items, representatives from all the charities, our sponsors, our board of directors, our volunteer leaders, and the many people who paid to be there. It was beautiful inside the tent. The only drawback was how cold it was. It was so cold, we had to pay for many heaters to be placed inside the tent, just to keep people remotely comfortable. This was event hell. The next couple of days didn't get any better.

As our Sunday night headliner, the legendary group from New Orleans, the Neville Brothers, played, it was 38 degrees. Not the kind of weather you want the third weekend in May. Because of this, The Neville Brothers were playing for a very sparse crowd. This happened on both nights. The cold weather played a huge role in the severe lack of the walk-up business we always depended on to save the event. After four in the afternoon each day, nobody else showed up. Our show was running smoothly, the food was great, the people were enjoying themselves but unfortunately we didn't have enough people come through the gates. We were in serious trouble. More trouble than we'd ever experienced before with Heart & Soul. As the weekend went along, all I could think of was that there was no way we'd be able to pay our expenses, let alone send money to the charities. It was brutal.

After the event, we were faced with the daunting task of contacting many of our vendors and working out payment arrangements. We simply did not have the money to pay them. Some of them were there, so they saw the same thing we did. Whether they were there or not, the result was still the same. For the first time in the history of Heart & Soul, we were in debt, and a lot of it. We could send nothing to our charities.

Among all the board and volunteer leaders, we dubbed our 2002 event "The Perfect Storm." The combination of Camp Heartland leaving us, the weather, the national artists not bringing in as many people as we had hoped, counting on our usual walk-up crowd to save the day, and some poor decisions caused us to fail despite our best intentions.

There was one more reason why it didn't work that year. It's not anything that you can touch or see, but it's just as real. The three charities we chose just didn't touch me the way Camp Heartland did in the beginning. They all did great work and were worthy of support, so it should have worked. However, I wasn't passionate about these charities. While I'm not the only person who dictates how the event goes, I am the face of the event. I think I didn't put on a very good face that year.

Personally, I was so focused on trying to take care of everything, put on a brave face and run a smooth show, that I overlooked the reason I started the whole thing in the first place. I did it because I thought I could make a difference and that was all that mattered. Although our charities were great charities, I didn't attempt to make a connection with them like I did with Camp Heartland. One of the reasons people joined my effort initially was because they could tell I was passionate in what I was doing. I lost that passion in 2002.

In 2001, I remember receiving a resignation letter from one of the board members who was with me from the beginning. She ended her letter stating she was inspired to be involved, especially in the "early days." That letter really upset me at the time. It felt like a slap in the face. But as I thought about it, she was right. I lost my way from those early days too. Now, Kristi would strongly disagree with that since she saw what I went through each year trying to do this event. But a fact is a fact. My perspective had changed. I had tunnel vision on all the details and lost my focus on why I started it in the first place. For me, it was that simple and realizing it was a bitter pill to swallow.

The board of directors for Heart & Soul faced a difficult decision. Do we file for bankruptcy? Do we dismantle the event and walk away? Or do we face our situation head-on and work on a solution? Thankfully, the integrity of the board members showed itself. The decision was made to stay in close contact with all the vendors we had an outstanding debt with and slowly, sometimes painfully slowly, find a way to pay our debt. Heart & Soul would learn from the hard lessons we were taught a few weeks before. We would not permit ourselves to make the same assumptions we used to. All bets were off. We put ourselves in defensive mode and settled into our foxholes. Where our focus used to be was finding any way to raise money for a charity, our only goal now was to pay back our debt and pray everyday that one of our vendors wouldn't take us to court for being faulty on our bill to them.

From negotiating with the vendors, opportunities arose to use our 501c3 status to assist other organizations to save money. Sending money to Heart & Soul, therefore, slowly got us back on track. This took a very long time. So long, we had to cancel our 2003 event because of the size of our outstanding debt. In 2004, we were getting closer and actually had a seriously reduced budget to do some kind of Heart & Soul event. But because of problems getting event and board of directors insurance for the event, we had to eventually cancel all proposed events in 2004. That was very disappointing, but necessary.

Heart & Soul could not risk another year of not being able to pay our bills. It was decided we would have to wait until 2005 to do an event.

While I'm not happy about not being able to do Heart & Soul for two consecutive years, I am very proud of another statement we made while we were out of service. We didn't run or hide from our debts. We maintained a solid and strong relationship with our vendors. We stayed in touch with them. We worked with them, and they worked with us. This method of negotiation and reason will serve the event well in the future. Our work in the past helped a lot of children in need. The machine is set up to do it again. We will come back and it will be because the pride of all the members of the board of directors for Heart & Soul wouldn't let it end with us filing for bankruptcy.

Each fundraiser has some basic elements: the incident that happened to give reason to the fundraiser, the call to action of the supporters of the cause, and the actual revenue being raised. The last element, although equally as important as the others, was convincing the donors, the attendees, and the participants that the fundraiser is a means to an eventual end. For a benefit such as children's cancer or Muscular Dystrophy as an example, it's understood that the cure, while getting closer each year, is not something that you expect to happen a few weeks after you donate your time.

Some fundraisers that musicians are asked to do are based on awareness of a cause or political movement. The results of this type of fundraiser are not tangible; you can't hold it in your hands. Most of the time it makes you feel good that you lent your name to a cause you believe in. It has been my experience that a sizable portion of fundraisers that musicians do is for

We give and give

other musicians. There are benefits for musicians because some band had its gear stolen. Some are for musicians who had unfortunately experienced the untimely death of their spouse and are now raising a family on their own. Some are for musicians who get in some type of accident and find themselves in the emergency room or have a lengthy hospital stay with no way to pay the hospital bill. It can be tough living as a musician. You spend so much time on your creative side that sometimes you forget about your practical side. The pursuit of mastering your instrument, improving your singing, improving your writing skills and promoting yourself means nothing if you don't take some time to take care of the things that give you stability.

If you're a teenage band, or a band in your early twenties, I can see some rationale in letting the boring stuff slide. When you're that young, you're indestructible. I felt I was at that age. But when you become a veteran in this business and you don't take care of these things, some questions need to be asked.

What stops a musician from insuring him- or herself medically or professionally? As someone who's performed at fundraisers and also as someone who was the recipient of a fundraiser, I felt a new thought process was necessary. Is doing benefits actually helping, or does the musical community need to focus on aspects that can better prepare them for eventual and almost certain incidents that will cause them professional, mental, or physical inconvenience. Two incidents defined for me the need for a new way of thinking.

There was a time in the early '90s where Mick Sterling and the Stud Brothers were performing every Sunday, Tuesday, Wednesday, and Thursday nights in the Twin Cities, as well as weekend dates and outdoor summer festival shows. We were working a lot for a local band. Although we were a ten-piece band, which meant money was split ten ways, we were still doing quite well for a local band. Things were going very smoothly until I received a phone call from our tech at the time. As I picked up the phone, I heard the shaky voice of our tech, who told me in a voice that was barely decipherable, that his trailer with all of the band's gear had been stolen. It had been parked in a fenced lot near his house. When he went to pick up the gear with his truck, the trailer was gone. We had a gig at the Fine Line in Minneapolis that night. The situation wasn't pretty.

I tried to calm him down and keep things on an even keel. As I hung up, I needed to reach the rest of the band immediately to tell them the news that the drums, guitar and bass amps, and all the keyboards had been stolen. As you can imagine, the reaction was, to put it kindly, artistically descriptive. The next few gigs the band played on lesser gear just to get the gigs done each night. We did the customary calling of police departments and music stores to see if the gear had been turned in or perhaps pawned. We received no news about our gear. It was nowhere to be found. To make matters worse, none of the players had insurance on their gear.

As a band leader, I never insisted on getting group insurance for our gear. I always thought it was too expensive. What became clear to me was that while blame should be on the person who stole our gear, blame needed to be placed on each member of our band and myself. There was no excuse for musicians who had been playing as long as we have to not insure ourselves professionally. Our losses were $20,000 to $30,000 in gear. Who was going to pay for that, our tech guy? He didn't have the money to do that. We had no agreement with him on paper that said if something was stolen it was his responsibility.

It was a handshake deal. He was our tech guy. We trusted him to bring the gear. It wasn't his fault anyway. He locked the trailer. Someone just really wanted that trailer and did whatever it took to steal it. Whether the thief knew the gear was in there when the trailer was stolen is uncertain. If he just wanted the trailer, he got a huge bonus with what was in it.

To try and resolve this, a benefit was thrown in our honor at The Cabooze. A lot of bands played for free, and we received donations at the door to help us pay for our gear. It was a very kind gesture. It was great to hang out with other musicians. The fans were great. I was grateful for the help. But I was unsatisfied too. Not because of the effort and goodwill from everybody, but the entire concept seemed flawed to me.

The other incident that made an impression on me was something that happened to another local musician. He had been on his bicycle one day and someone behind him ran into him on the path he was riding, causing him to flip off the bike and fly about ten feet forward. He wound up unconscious for a while with lots of bruises and scrapes and a broken jaw. Needless to say, he needed a trip to the emergency room.

This accident wound up costing him nearly $12,000 in hospital bills. He was going to face this alone because he didn't have any health insurance. Unfortunately, that scenario is all too common for people who work in the music industry. Not only was he beat up and unable to do some gigs, which was money out of his pocket, he was facing a $12,000 hospital bill.

It's situations like this that the musical community of the Twin Cities comes together to help their own. This person had a lot of friends in the music scene, so asking them to help him wasn't going to be an issue. Helping him find a way to pay for some of these bills was the top priority. However, after talking to him I wanted to use this event to promote something else. I wanted this benefit to be used as an effort to make musicians start waking up a bit.

There needed to be some way to get musicians to start thinking of ways to prepare for accidents that land them in the hospital or for their gear getting stolen. I was more than happy to put together a benefit for my band member, but that benefit needed to do more than just be a vehicle to raise money. The amount of money that is raised at events like this has always been an issue for me. At many of the benefits most musicians are asked to do, the amount of money needed to be raised is in the low $20,000 range and sometimes as high as $100,000 to cover medical costs. How can a benefit that musicians throw together at a bar possibly come close to covering these expenses? You'd have to do ten to fifteen benefits to cover all the expenses. You can only get people to come together once, maybe twice if you're lucky. After you make $2,000 to $3,000, maybe $5,000 from the benefit at the bar, where do you go for the rest of the money? Somehow, we have to find a way to make the goals at these benefits attainable at a reachable level. The only way to do that is to find a way for musicians to prepare for these things by getting insurance.

I wanted to help find a way to help my friend pay back his hospital bills, but I also wanted to use the event to raise awareness about finding a way to help musicians out of situations like this. I called it The Turning Point Insurance Cooperative.

The concept of Turning Point was to find an outlet for musicians to gain medical insurance and gear insurance for under $100 a month. The medical insurance would be the kind of insurance that had a $2,500 deductible with one hundred percent of the remaining bill, up to $5 million, covered. Granted, that's a high deductible, but at least it's some kind of insurance instead of no insurance. That $2,500 is also a reachable amount to do a benefit for. If the musician gets in an accident and has a huge hospital bill staring at him or her, their musician friends can still get together and do a benefit. This way, they'd only be looking at a $2,500 bill to cover the deductible instead of tens of thousands of dollars, a total that is completely unreachable for the majority of players in club land.

The other issue for musicians is getting their gear stolen. Because our gear had been stolen a couple of years prior, I was sensitive to this. It happens to a lot of bands. Our remedy is always the same. Either go out and buy new stuff, bitch and whine about how much it sucks, or have a benefit thrown that will more often than not fall far short of the total needed to replace your gear. The solution is to get gear insurance. The perception has always been that gear insurance was far too expensive to have it make sense. After all, the chances that your gear will get stolen are far less than it wouldn't get stolen. In a short-term way of thinking, it makes more sense not to get insurance. All that is well and good until you're on the receiving end of some cold-blooded theft of your livelihood. Then you start thinking differently. I wanted Turning Point to address this.

I talked to the representative for Michael Monroe, a very well-established and respected acoustic artist for many years in the Minnesota music scene. His wife, Deb, told me about an insurance company called Clarion Musical Insurance based in New York. She said Michael had been with them for years. The rates were fantastic and, best of all, this insurance company covered all the scenarios that musicians find themselves in. If your gear gets stolen in your trailer when you're on the road, it's covered. If your gear gets damaged by an amp falling on it, it's covered. The list went on and on. It made so much sense. I wanted to get this information out there.

My goal was to find a way for musicians to have an outlet to cover themselves medically and professionally for under $100 a month. That's not a huge amount of money. It's definitely workable. Turning Point was able to do that. Another aspect of it was that I didn't want to have a certain amount of musicians to sign up for this before it could kick in. The rates were individual. It would be their insurance alone. The musicians would be dealing with two different insurance agents, but at least their total, if they decided to get both, would most likely be under $100 per month.

The Turning Point benefit had seventeen bands and artists perform. All the artists were given information about Turning Point. We talked about it on stage often. We encouraged musicians to find out about it and start taking steps to insure themselves. I knew it was a long shot and an uphill battle but I felt like it was worth attempting.

What followed Turning Point was a thundering roar of indifference. I did talk to some musicians who said they pursued things. A few of them came up to me and said they had insured themselves for the first time in their lives. That made me feel great, but I wish more musicians had taken advantage of this opportunity.

I'm sure the vast majority of the musicians who performed at the event or heard of it, never did anything to change their situation. You can't force anybody to do anything, especially musicians.

The musical community of the Twin Cities is compassionate and ready to help people in need. That's always a good thing. I'm proud to be a part of it. Compassion is as valid an ingredient in any successful benefit or movement as finding people with financial and sponsorship connections to get your message out. All events need a few special people who get what you're trying to do. The pursuit to do something positive is a powerful magnet. You need a spark. I've been fortunate to be a spark for a few efforts, and I'm grateful for it. It's our opportunity to acknowledge and celebrate our good fortune to be able to make a living playing music. As Chuck Berry so proudly exclaimed, "Hail, hail rock and roll."

We give and give

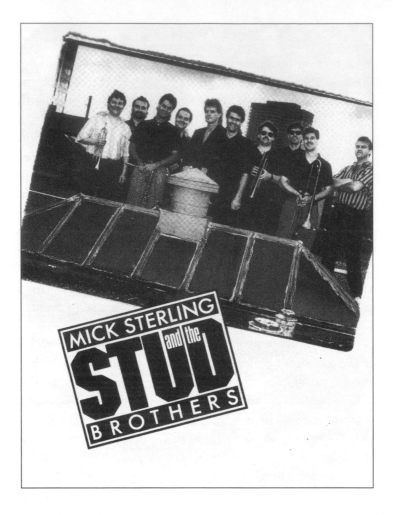

This shot was taken on the roof of some building on Nicollet Mall.
This was late '80s, early '90s, I can't remember. We were just pups
up there. Things were just starting to get hot around town for us at
that time. Most of the guys in the band in this picture left the band
a few months later because things were clearly out of the realm of a
part-time band. It got a little hectic. (Left to Right: Bernie Edstrom—
Trumpet, John Kuczek—Bass, Doug Kuehn—Sax, Tate Ferguson—
Guitar, Layne Bender—Sax, Me, Bob Hallgrimson—Trumpet,
Mark Moran—Hammond Organ, King Steven Pikal—Trombone,
Dan Eidem—Drums)

It puts hair on your chest

he voices we hear today that are so distinctive and original
are, more than likely, not as original as you may
think. While it's true that many of the leading artists
in our lifetime set the standard for the kind of music that
followed, I propose that, deep in their guts, they would
admit to using their influences to mold the sound you
hear today. Some artists openly admit to their influences.
Some don't. Most of the time, all you have to do is listen
to their music and you know whom they listened to when
they were young. How artists, either internationally
known or locally based, deal with their influences is
another defining aspect of each artist. The combination
of influences and being lucky enough to witness and
acknowledge inspirational moments that cross your path
not only defines an artist, but it comes close to complet-
ing the moment a club-goer, concert-goer, or album-lis-
tener experiences.

When people see me perform in the Twin Cities, I
think it's pretty obvious to most people out there who
influenced me. It would be great to tell you that everything I do on stage and in the studio is completely unique
and original. That would be a lie. I wish I could say that
my influences are so subtle that they could barely be

noticed, but they aren't. They guide me on stage each night. They guide me when I sit down and write lyrics to a song. They guide me when I open my mouth and sing an original or cover song. Every time I sing, I eventually channel a combination of Springsteen, Southside Johnny, and Elton, whether I'm trying to do it or not. As the years have progressed, my own voice has taken up a larger percentage of what my audience hears, but I know what's beneath it. Springsteen, Southside Johnny, and Elton are my support system. For whatever reason, all of them came into my young life at the time that the mental part of me locked into it, and the physical part of the actual workings of my larynx and voice box could handle singing like them.

I never get offended when people say they see my influences in what I do. I figure I'm lucky to be influenced by some of the giants I actually like. It could be worse. I could be influenced by the Bay City Rollers, Starland Vocal Band, and Poco. That would truly be my version of a daily dose of fresh hell. It comforts me to know that my path is not that different from well-established artists in popular music. I'm certainly not putting myself in this same category, but you'll get the idea. The Beatles had Buddy Holly and Little Richard. Bob Dylan had Woody Guthrie. The Stones had Muddy Waters and other blues legends. Tom Petty had The Byrds. Prince had James Brown and Sly Stone. Lenny Kravitz had Prince and Hendrix. Stevie Ray Vaughan had Hendrix and Albert Collins. And the list goes on and on. Everything derives from something else. The artists, either locally or nationally, who blatantly steal from their influences (and what you watch or listen to is a carbon copy of those influences), will more than likely fail or wallow in mediocrity. The ones that stand out are the artists who embrace their influences and use them to form their own interpretation.

I find myself in a balancing act with my influences and my own voice. When I find myself there, I have to dig a bit deeper and remember the influences and inspirations that educated me.

Inspiration comes in many forms. Sometimes inspiration comes in the form of shame, humiliation, and embarrassment. There are many clichés that apply when these moments happen. I'm grateful for those moments now, but at the time they were painful. None of them were life-threatening or career-ending scenarios, but did play a role in how I perform to this day.

When I was in seventh grade, I auditioned and got the role of the Artful Dodger in the musical "Oliver" at Armstrong Senior High School in Plymouth. In eighth grade, I got the role of the oldest son, Prince Chulalongkorn, in "The King and I." Each year in school, every time I auditioned for something, I seemed to get the lead role for a child. It wasn't something I was particularly excited about auditioning for. I just went in and did what I did. Luckily, what I was doing was good enough to make the play. My lucky streak with getting lead roles in plays ended when I was in the eleventh grade.

Believe me, I'm thinking what you're thinking. This story isn't very tough or mean. I wish I could tell you that my lucky streak ended when someone tried to jump me at the audition, or I was beat to within an inch of my life by some schoolyard drama hooligan, but it just didn't go down that way. Despite the lack of drama, what happened in the eleventh grade concerning a musical at Armstrong Senior High School, opened my eyes and slapped me around a bit.

I failed to get a lead role in the musical "Hello, Dolly" at Armstrong in eleventh grade. I did get a role as a dancer and in the chorus. That had never happened to me before. Because of that, I wasn't very excited about being in the show. I would show up to rehearsals, but I would rarely listen. I would sing in the chorus, but I really didn't know the words. I would mix into

It puts hair on your chest

the background and mumble the words. At the dance rehearsals, I would never watch the choreographer teach us. I picked up on a few of the moves, but I was way in the back, so I never really thought he was even paying attention to me. Basically, I was floating and wasting everybody's time. It didn't concern me though. I thought I was unimportant. I was in the chorus. If I didn't deliver, someone else would. Plus I was feeling a bit sorry for myself. The combination of all those things led me to my eventual awakening.

As the show was a couple of weeks away, the male part of the chorus had to sing and dance the famous waiter scene from "Hello, Dolly." Lots of dancing, lots of jumping around, lots of intricate moves, lots of large platters you had to spin around, as all the waiters do their thing before Dolly walks down the steps to sing the signature song. In the crowd for this performance were all the cast members, the choreographer, the director, and some other school administrators. As the music began and the lights went up, all of us in the chorus soon found out that we were in serious trouble.

None of us knew the song. None of us knew the dance moves. It was a disaster. The cast members were upset with us. The director was disgusted. The choreographer was humiliated. Our performance that day proved to the director, the musical director, and the choreographer that we had just wasted three weeks of their life trying to teach us this scene.

I wasn't used to disappointing people. I wasn't used to failing. I did both that day and it really hit me hard. I was no better than a spoiled-rotten punk that day. I deserved every bad thing that happened that day because I did nothing prior to that to deserve any type of praise for my efforts.

When I got back to school that Monday morning, I immediately found the director and the musical director. I told them how sorry I was for not doing what I was supposed to be doing.

I admitted that since I was in the chorus, I wasn't paying attention. I admitted that my lack of attention to matters was due to the fact that I wasn't the lead and I didn't think my contribution would be that important. I admitted to them that I failed myself and my cast members. I also promised them that day that I would change my ways and learn from the humiliation of the last rehearsal.

The following rehearsals found all of us working harder. Some of this is naturally due to the fact that with any show, as opening night draws nearer, things just start coming together. But for me, that humiliating rehearsal proved to me that what you contribute is what you get back.

Sometimes shame is a great learning tool. A lot of parents these days do everything they can to have their kids avoid feeling shame or embarrassment. In sporting events, the parents and the league officials find ways to have little kids not really lose. As long as they tried, that should be good enough. Well, in real life it's not good enough to just try. People lose in real life. If you don't learn from losing, shame, and embarrassment as a kid, how can you deal with it when you're an adult?

When I perform in clubs, there are many times during the night when I'm not the focal point. I want to direct the attention over to the person who is soloing. But just because someone is soloing and I'm not the focal point, doesn't mean my contribution on that stage at that moment isn't important. I still have a job to do as a team player. I have to focus on the audience and the soloist at the same time. I have to project the image to the people in the audience that I'm enjoying what I'm doing. It has to be believable. The audience sees everything.

If they see me being disinterested or bored, that's what they'll remember. If I project boredom onstage, it's a disservice to the rest of the band. As the front man, I would be failing at my job if I didn't follow through the entire show. It doesn't matter if I play in a little hole in the wall or on a large outdoor stage for thousands of people; the principle remains exactly the same. I learned that in high school. I'm grateful I'm not jaded enough to forget it.

There are times when inspiration for your musical career can come from a nonmusical source. Right after my daughter was born, I found myself out of a job.

I wasn't working in a band at the time. Financially, it was pretty scary for my wife and me. I found out about an opportunity to do some work as a house painter for some new home construction sites in the northern metro area of the Twin Cities. At the time, to save more money, my wife and I agreed to be caretakers in an apartment complex in uptown Minneapolis. One of my caretaking duties was to paint the apartments when tenants moved out. I've done a lot of painting in my life, so I figured a job as a house painter was something I could do. It was a five-day-a-week job, eight hours a day, and I'd be paid weekly. This job could solve some problems. Little did I know that it would also cause me some more financial worries and clear things up for me at the same time. As soon as I started my first day as a house painter, I knew I was out of my element. Among my longtime friends and people who work with me, it's well known that I'm a complete idiot when it comes to building things, fixing cars, fixing things around the house, trying to back a U-Haul trailer into a spot, and many other things that most men naturally know how to do. I thought house painting would be one of the things that didn't belong on this list of male duties, but apparently I was horribly mistaken.

I had no idea how hard house painters actually work. I had no idea how fast they actually painted. I also had no idea how bad I'd be at the job. The person who was responsible for me was known around the construction site as the best and fastest painter on their team. He was also known as having little patience for people who couldn't keep up. What I quickly found out was that he saw right through me. I was a joke to him, but he wasn't laughing. Neither was I. Every morning, I came to the construction site hoping I would do a better job. Not because I had a desire to be a better house painter, but because I desperately needed this job. The foreman of the painting company was the father of one of my wife's high school friends, so I had that on my side. But each day I worked, it became abundantly clear that I wasn't working out. I dreaded going to work every day. I made mistakes. I was working too slowly to keep up with the rest of the painters. Plus, my immediate supervisor was basically just giving me dirty looks every time he saw me. If it would have been up to him, I would have been fired before the second day. Because the foreman was the father of a high school friend, I didn't get fired until the end of the second week. I was grateful to eventually get fired because I sucked at this job. The ride home from the site to tell my wife and new daughter, (who couldn't talk yet but I still talked to her) that I was out of a job again was something I was not looking forward to.

As I was riding home that day, I had an epiphany. I was about to come home unemployed with a wife and new baby daughter. I had no prospects. No Plan B. No savings. Despite that, something became so obvious to me. Realizing it lessened my load a bit, I was still out of a job, but now it didn't seem so bad. What I realized was that I needed to stop messing around and get serious about what I wanted to do. I needed to get myself back to playing music. Not just part time, but full time. I realized that just as it was perfectly obvious that I was not a painter, it was also obvious to me that my tormentor on the job site couldn't do what I do. He paints. I can sing Southside Johnny songs. He paints fast and accurately. I paint slowly and sloppily. To each his own. Everybody has the things they do and the things they don't do.

While it was embarrassing to me that I couldn't handle a house-painting job, it certainly wasn't a professional blow to my manhood. It was more of a financial blow to my manhood at the time. This situation just proved to me that I needed to focus my efforts on finding a way to make money doing what I really knew how to do: make music. It didn't happen right away. I eventually landed another waiter job to pay the bills, but the wheels were in motion. I had to find a way to make a living playing music my reality. Eventually, it happened.

I've been able to work with some great people in the Twin Cities during my twenty-plus years of performing. During this time, I've had the pleasure of witnessing things that inspired me to be a better performer. Sometimes what I witnessed made me want to stop being a performer because I knew I couldn't reach that level. Most of the time though, these moments provided me with the stimulus to improve what I do.

When you see somebody doing something really well, you have the opportunity to take it a couple of ways. Either you can react defiantly and let jealousy and envy convince yourself that what you've seen really isn't that impressive, or you can take the position that someone just taught you the right way to do something. I have faith in my ability, but I've never been foolish enough to ignore, because of spite or envy, someone doing something extraordinary. When these moments happen, you have to soak it in and eventually apply it to what you do.

One night in the early '80s, at the now defunct Union Bar in Minneapolis, I was among a crowd of fifteen to twenty people seeing a band called Ipso Facto. Ipso Facto and another band in town, Shangoya, were the two leading reggae bands in the Twin Cities at the time. Both put on great shows. Ipso Facto was hot at the time. Their shows were well known for being great parties. The groove was huge. They drew big crowds and they were very hot.

On this particular winter night the weather was brutal. Because of that, the crowd for the first set was well below to what the band was accustomed. I used to love the Union Bar. Great sight lines, big sound system, the low end could shake your chest. It had a great history in the Minneapolis music scene. I was hoping to witness a huge crowd and Ipso Facto doing its thing. When I walked into the bar, the crowd was not what I expected. However, what I did find out that night was how powerful Ipso Facto really was.

Fronted by Wain McFarlane, Ipso Facto began the night just as I had hoped for. The groove was deep and huge. The band was tight. As someone who was just beginning his club career, I came in looking for ways to improve what I do. What concerned me was the size of the crowd. I didn't think much excitement could be generated because of the small crowd. I couldn't have been more wrong.

Sometime after the second or third song, Wain McFarlane and the rest of the Ipso Facto band took matters into their own hands. Because of the type of band they were and their professionalism, they ignored the fact that there were only fifteen people in the room. They ignored the fact that it was just the first set. What they chose to do was deliver on an unspoken promise. It was beautiful to witness.

Wain took those fifteen people and made them his own. He lifted us up. He got us out of our chairs. He took away any self-conscious feeling anybody may have had. He convinced all of us that night that it was our duty to get into it. He convinced us, (even if in reality, they weren't excited at all) that the band was really happy to be playing for fifteen people. In my eyes, he was the greatest front man I'd ever seen. I was so appreciative that he considered the fact that all fifteen of us had gone out of our way to drive through a bitterly cold and snowy night in Minneapolis to see Ipso Facto. I firmly believe that all fifteen of

It puts hair on your chest

us would have forgiven Ipso Facto that night if they'd just messed around that first set and not delivered a knockout punch performance. We didn't expect it, but thankfully for all of us there that night, they did. Wain and his band moved me that night. It inspired me. It's something that I remember every time I play. It doesn't matter how many people are in the crowd. It doesn't matter where you're playing. A job is a job. If my job is to be a front man of a great band, it's my job to make sure that the people who are there experience a strong front man and a great band. Just like anybody who takes pride in their job, I take pride in mine when I know I gave it all I had. Sometimes you give it all you have when you really don't want to. The quick reply to that is, so what and stop whining. Wain McFarlane taught me that night that being a professional performer means you have to go the whole way, even if the venue or circumstance falls far short of what you want it to be.

About this same time, I was fortunate enough to have a gig in the back room of the now defunct room called Mr. Nib's in Minneapolis. The club had just remodeled, providing name bands in town with a huge stage and a big sound system. The newer bands in town had the opportunity to play in the back room, a much smaller version of the main stage. It didn't matter to us at the time, it was a gig in a Minneapolis club. We were hungry to do anything we could get.

On this night, the Doug Maynard Band was playing on the main stage inside Nib's. Our bands started at the same time, so I wasn't able to see them until our break. When I did emerge from our cavern in the back of the room, I experienced something I'll never forget. It was, to this day, the greatest club band I'd ever seen. It was the biggest, baddest, funkiest, grittiest bar band I'd experienced.

The lineup of the Doug Maynard Band at the time was full of people I'd never met before. I'd heard of some of them, but

I'd never heard any of them play before. The band was led by a man who was very quiet and subdued, and not very large in stature. His movements were very slight when he sang. In fact, he barely moved. His eyes seemed constantly closed. He dressed very casually. It was obvious to me that his intention was not to dazzle you with his showmanship. What was also obvious to me was that as soon as he started singing, I knew that I was witnessing one of the most soulful and powerful things I'd ever seen.

Sharing the vocal duties in the Doug Maynard Band were two gorgeous women who seemed to move in tandem so naturally that no choreography was needed. Not only did these women look incredible on stage, when they sang they made the fact of their sexiness seem insignificant. This was quite a feat, because the two women singing—Melanie Rosales and Margaret Cox—were really damn sexy. When Melanie sang, she had the raspy, soulful twang that reminded you a bit of Bonnie Raitt, but not enough to bug you. She was something else. Margaret Cox had such a powerful and crystal clear delivery that it was a great contrast to Melanie. Margaret seemed to be channeling Chaka Khan when she sang, but again, not enough to bug me. Bonnie and Chaka were in Melanie and Margaret, and I was glad they were there. The combination of Margaret and Melanie complimented what Doug was doing. When they all sang together, it was perfection to me.

The other person in the band who made a huge impression on me was the drummer, Bobby Vandell. I'd never seen anyone play the drums like Bobby. I definitely had never seen anyone hit the drums so hard. It was clear he wanted to be seen. I didn't think that was a bad thing. I thought it was really powerful. It was clear to me that Bobby wanted attention drawn his way, but not to the point of overshadowing what Doug and the rest of the band was doing. The groove Bobby

It puts hair on your chest

laid down on all the songs in the Doug Maynard Band was so big and deep, it was inspiring.

Back in those days, I watched Bobby from afar. I never spoke to him; I was too intimidated. When my band, Mick Sterling and the Stud Brothers, was starting to make a buzz in town, I would see him from time to time in other projects. The first time I played with Bobby was at an outdoor gig in Mankato, Minnesota, called The People's Fair. This particular gig found my band in substitute hell. I had a lot of subs in the horn section and a couple in the rhythm section. Fortunately for me, one of them was Bobby. As soon we hit the first song, I heard the Bobby Vandell that I heard back in the '80s at Mr. Nib's. What Bobby did that day was not an uncommon occurrence. Whenever Bobby found himself in a situation where he was sitting in or subbing, more often than not—as it did in the Doug Maynard Band—the dynamic of the band changed. "I wasn't intentionally trying to steal someone's gig, but I could walk into a situation, schmooze, and get to know the guys so that I wasn't a threat to them," says Vandell. "More times than not, the band would sound better with me sitting in. That's what happened with Doug Maynard. I initially played congas for them and occasionally I would play the drums. Every time I played the drums, they seemed to liked it better."

More than a decade later, the same thing happened to me in Mankato. As soon as my gig at The People's Fair started and I heard Bobby play, I knew it was something I wanted to hear more often. In a few months, I made a big changeover in the band. Hiring Bobby as my drummer in the band was the first thing I did. There are just some people you meet while you do your job that you identify with more than others. I think with Bobby, I felt that connection back then. I still feel it today.

One of the things that I identify with him is the actual way he drums. As someone who took drum lessons for years as a kid, I had that in common with him. I could nail the paradiddles and flamecues. I could play the seven and thirteen stroke rolls on my snare drum and practice pad and read the Haskell Harr drum book like a pro, but I wanted to do more. Unfortunately, once I entered seventh grade, I trailed off on my drum lessons because of sports and doing theater, so I never started playing on an actual drum set. The first time I saw Bobby play was how I visualized I would play if I played a drum set. It was weird, but it was real to me.

Bobby Vandell had his first gig in eighth grade in front a school assembly of eight hundred people. He played drums and he sang the Solomon Burke song, "Turn on Your Love Light." "It would be fifteen years until I would play for a crowd as large as that again," joked Vandell. He performed with his childhood and lifelong friend, the late and great bassist, Doug Nelson. Getting the taste of playing rock and roll was a defining moment for Vandell. "The first way it defined me as a teenager was the confidence it gives you," he says. "You can't get it from anywhere else. Suddenly you're in a group. In a way, it's like a gang. Your peers are admiring you. You're making a little bit of money. What could build your confidence up more than that? Plus you get attention from the opposite sex. I suppose you can get it playing sports, it's just different being a musician. That feeling of confidence never left me."

Bobby moved to the Twin Cities and started performing in many different bands, averaging two to three bands a year. Many times, the bands' gigs would coincide, so it kept him very busy. One of the bands that was hot around this time was a band called Passage, which quite often featured Doug Maynard as the lead vocalist. For a moment in time, Doug was not singing with Passage, so they were looking for another vocalist to fill his slot. One night, a couple of the members of Passage saw Bobby perform with another band. They asked him to become their lead singer. Bobby agreed. His first night performing with Passage was stressful. To make matters even more stressful, Doug Maynard showed up and sat at the table right in front of him to check him out. "He vibed me to death," says Vandell of Doug Maynard, "I just tried to shut it out and do the gig. It was intimidating, but I got through it. We eventually became friends."

Vandell eventually became the drummer for the Doug Maynard Band. The band became one of the biggest draws in the Twin Cities back in the early '80s. Praise was coming from all around for the band. Critical praise was plentiful for Doug Maynard and his distinctive style. For most people, complimenting what you do would provide a sense of comfort and satisfaction. For Doug, it wasn't always that easy. "Any little thing that would happen to Doug at a rehearsal or gig or wherever, it would take his confidence away from him," says Vandell. Battling those insecurities and other issues from prior to his performing days was something that Doug Maynard battled with all of his performing life. For band members like Vandell, it was something they had to deal with every time they performed.

As the Doug Maynard Band wound down, Vandell saw the opportunity to move to L. A. and acted on it. While in L. A., he soon found out that while the weather was great, the gigs were hard to come by and the competition was very stiff. "Working in L. A., there were no PAs in the clubs like there are now," says Vandell. "The commutes to the gigs were just ridiculous, sometimes seventy to eighty miles to a gig. Fifty dollars a night was common pay. If you subbed out a gig, you were likely to be replaced by Stevie Wonder's drummer or the Doobie Brothers' drummer or any other type of national artist's drummer. Some of the finest musicians in the nation would do a gig for $50. They'd pay their drum tech $150 to do a $50 gig. It was cool though. You get opportunities to work with people. It was a really tough thing to work out there. You just don't succeed in L. A. overnight."

While Bobby was living in L. A., he received a call from Steve Greenberg, the writer and producer of the song "Funkytown," to become the drummer for the band Lipps Inc. "Funkytown" was a huge hit around the world. The song was being played all over the place, except the city where it originated, Minneapolis. "I called all my friends back in Minneapolis to tell them I got hired to play in this band with this huge hit, and nobody in town knew who I was talking about," recalls Vandell. "'Funkytown' was a single from a black-oriented sound. A black-oriented single just didn't market well at that time." That soon changed. Vandell moved back to Minneapolis for good in the mid '80s. He came back a changed man. "The main thing L. A. did for me was it gave me a lot of confidence when I came back to the Twin Cities. I never would have become a band leader without working L. A.," says Vandell. "I just came back different. The musicians I worked with in Minneapolis seemed to notice I came back stronger. I think people got out of the way because I knew where was going. I just felt strong when I got back because L. A. made me strong."

Once back in town, Vandell became the leader of a band he played with before heading out to L. A., the T. C. Jammers. He was also in the first incarnation of the Dr. Mambo's Combo, the Monday and Tuesday night house band at Bunkers Music Bar and Grill in Minneapolis. Both bands featured some of the best players in town, and both bands featured a multiethnic stage presence. For Vandell, the opportunity to play with a racially mixed lineup was very important. The satisfaction of that reality runs deep within Vandell for many reasons. "I have worked with more black people than most. I consider it an honor," he says. "I grew up listening to so much great music. The roots of

It puts hair on your chest

all pop music come from black musicians: Sam Cooke, Aretha, Sam and Dave, Ray Charles. To work with people of color has been a great honor. It's been even more honorable to have black musicians respect me when I've been the only white musician in the band. "Lets face it, white musicians got a great deal from black musicians. For black musicians to respect me is an enormous compliment."

Having performed thousands of gigs in his career, there are many highlights for Vandell. But one gig in particular stands out. It was playing drums in one of the pick-up bands that greet Chuck Berry every time he rolls up to the stage in a different city. "It was such an honor to play with Chuck Berry," says Vandell. "It was such an honor to sit with Chuck Berry in his Lincoln Continental for ten minutes as Chuck is explaining to his pick-up band for the night what to play. I just kept thinking, everything I ever did in my life is worth it because right now I'm sitting in a car with one of the guys that invented rock and roll."

Currently, Vandell is performing as the drummer for Mick Sterling and the Stud Brothers, as well as the leader of the TC Jammers. The TC Jammers perform in clubs, as well as perform for corporate and private events, and occasionally wedding receptions. For local bands, the wide array of gigs you have the opportunity to do can be met with skepticism, or you could just be thankful for the work. Every musician likes to get paid. But sometimes, what you have to do to get paid being a working musician isn't exactly something you want the world to notice. Despite the fact that playing a wedding isn't the most musically stimulating thing, Vandell understands that he has to play a different role when the TC Jammers play a wedding, simply because he's the leader of the band. "As a leader, when I get a wedding gig, I deal with weeks of talking with the client, pampering them, getting songs for the first dance, the wedding party, and more," he says. "All the work that I put into the preparation eventually does pay off. Despite how I feel about it musically, as the leader, I do get some satisfaction when the client walks up to me and says they're happy.

"It has nothing to do with music, it has everything to do with doing your job right. It's satisfying. It's a lot of work, a lot of pressure and responsibility. People are spending a lot of money. My only job is to make them happy, not to play music I particularly enjoy. My job is to make the client happy. Now, I'd rather not have to play wedding gigs, but I do enjoy it when I do it well.

"You've got this big, cavernous thing between the clients' most important day of their lives and the least important night of the musician's life. Lets face it, there's not a musician alive that cares about going to play a wedding. I need to hire people that even if they're not enjoying playing, they at least act like they're enjoying it. It's a big responsibility as the leader of the band. When I play a wedding as a sideman and not the leader, I truly hate playing them. As a leader, I see it from a different perspective."

Bobby Vandell has been a leading force in the Twin Cities club scene for many years. His work as a drummer in the Twin Cities is one the most distinctive sounds in the long, proud tradition of the Minneapolis soul and R & B scene. While he's no different from any other musician in the sense that there are some nights that find him questioning why he keeps doing it, there are some things that will always ring true. "I heard a great phrase that describes what it feels like to be a musician," says Vandell. "Music gives you a chance to transcend your neighborhood. You can go beyond your environment that you were brought up in, to rise above it, look down and leave it. As a musician, that possibility always exists. There aren't many jobs out there that have the ability to do that."

It puts hair on your chest

Vandell also has some advice for younger musicians as well. "If the music isn't enough of a reward, don't do it. It's got to be that, that's all there is," proclaims Vandell. "Either music comes to you and chooses you, or it doesn't. Music chose me. I didn't have a choice in the matter."

A common theme for musicians, or in any competitive business setting, is that you assume things about people you've never met. If someone is a big fan of Twin Cities-based-singer-songwriter Mason Jennings, I'd naturally assume they wouldn't like the kind of music I produce. My style doesn't mesh with Mason Jennings' style, so I naturally make assumptions about Mason Jennings, as much as his fans would make assumptions about me. When the two worlds of musical styles occasionally collide, it always raises some eyebrows.

If Mason's fans knew that someone who plays music like Mick Sterling hangs out with Mason and is actually a great friend and someone Mason respects and admires, it would surprise and puzzle Mason's fans. My fans would be surprised too if the tables were turned. Strange but true.

Now the fact is, I enjoy and respect Mason Jennings' music, but I've never met him. He may like my music too, but since we've never met, I wouldn't know. The point is people want their favorite artists to associate with the kind of people whom we presume they should hang out with, namely people who like the same music and experience the same scene. Most of the time it works out like that. Occasionally, things get out of whack and things naturally just fall together. Maybe not as perfectly as a Reese's Peanut Butter Cup moment, but damn close to it.

I always think of how many people in the Twin Cities, in the country, and the world would gladly trade places with me every Thanksgiving at my in-laws' house when Lori Barbero walks through the door. As shocking as it will be to her fans, Lori Barbero is actually a dear family friend. To rub more salt on the wounds of Lori's fans, Lori and I actually like each other and have a lot in common. Our musical paths and styles are completely different, but it's a small town. We have a lot of the same friends in the business and we share a number of basic issues that all bands go through. Plus, she's just a cool person.

Because Lori grew up in the same neighborhood with my wife and her family, Lori is a part of our family. Through our conversations around the family table for nearly twenty years, and keeping track of her career via magazines and through her mom Rose Barbero, I have an enormous amount of respect for Lori. She's truly one of the finest ambassadors of the Minneapolis music scene. Her warmth, kindness, and world-renowned laugh have been, and still are, a welcome presence when touring artists come to Minneapolis. As the drummer and the leader of the innovative and trendsetting band Babes in Toyland, Lori has influenced countless bands around the country. What makes Lori so genuine is that she truly loves music— all kinds of music. As with every core belief and trait, Lori's love of music began when she was a child.

Lori Barbero's mind was blown when she was in the fifth grade at Page Elementary School in south Minneapolis. Many days after school, Lori would go to her friend Ann Hoff's house. Ann had older brothers. One day, her brothers were playing the Alice Cooper song "Halo of Lies."

"I just thought it was the coolest thing I've ever heard in my life," recalls Barbero. "I didn't know anything about drums or how they were set up, but I knew every single beat and I knew that sound. I knew I had to hit something, somewhere." Something about that song affected Lori deeply, it seemed to come to her out of nowhere.

"I'd heard tons of music before that, but that song was like an ode. It was so unbelievably heavy with all these different

It puts hair on your chest

things going on. It was the first time I noticed the drums and not just the vocals," she says. The method of celebration of her newfound quest was not particularly innovative or groundbreaking, but it definitely scratched a fifth-grader's itch in the late 60's version of a rock-and-roll itch.

"Every day we'd come home from school and go to Ann's house," recalls Barbero. "In her bedroom, she had two twin beds. We'd listen to that record and I would sing that song and jump from bed to bed, swinging my arms in the air to where the drums would be. I knew there were six different drum sounds, but I didn't know where each sound came from. I knew when I grew up, I was going to be a drummer. I didn't even know if there were girl drummers, I just knew I was going to be one."

The sheer joy of discovering music is powerful stuff and a memory that lingers your whole life.

"I actually saw Alice Cooper a couple of years ago and he played that song," says Barbero. "As soon as he played that song, the audience was invisible to me. The energy I was feeling was amazing. It totally took me back."

Lori spent her high school years in New York City. While there, she was exposed to all kinds of music, particularly a wide array of underground rock bands. She also was exposed to the influential CBGB's and other clubs that were showcasing bands that would eventually become critical and commercial successes around the world. While Lori's musical knowledge was expanding, she had yet to make the jump into actually performing herself.

When Lori moved back to Minneapolis, she got a job at a club called the Longhorn on 5th and Hennepin in downtown Minneapolis. For music lovers outside of the Twin Cities in the late '70s and early '80s, the Longhorn, along with Uncle Sam's, (which eventually became Sam's, which eventually morphed in to First Avenue and 7th Street Entry) were the two leading clubs that were showcasing underground, new wave, and punk music. Many artists who are household names now like the Police, Elvis Costello, Blondie, and many others performed at the Longhorn when they first came to the Twin Cities. For a period of time, Lori was a waitress at the Longhorn. It was there that the networking abilities of Lori Barbero kicked into full gear. Lori makes friends. She's friendly. All kinds of people like her. Musicians loved her, and she loved them. The Ambassador was in her element.

"The Longhorn was owned by a guy named Hartley Frank," says Barbero. "It was really one of the first clubs in town that was open to any music. Iggy Pop played there. The Plasmatics played there and many others." The Longhorn was not only a place for national artists to perform, it would have local house bands that would help to define the tone of the room. The Wednesday night house band back then was a band called The Suburbs, which eventually gained national attention and secured their legendary status in the Minneapolis music scene.

"I thought it was pretty cool. I was already going to CBGB's when I was in New York, so the Longhorn felt like home to me," says Barbero. "The Replacements would play at the club. Tommy Stinson was thirteen at the time I think, when they played in front of The Plasmatics. National and local bands of all types and talent levels played at the Longhorn. Influential Minneapolis-based bands like Husker Du and The Replacements rocked at the Longhorn and First Avenue. Those two bands became my favorite bands of all time. I just dearly love them. They became close friends and I saw every show they ever did back then."

Like all clubs, some bands stood out, some flopped. But the significance of the Longhorn in the past and First Avenue during

It puts hair on your chest

the same time and in the present day is one of the main reasons the Twin Cities is known to have a thriving music scene. In her early days at the Longhorn, Barbero saw something one night in the club that proved to be a pivotal moment her life.

"I watched Cindy Blum of NNB and Redhouse play drums at the Longhorn, First Avenue, and the Guthrie in one week," recalls Barbero. "I thought to myself, that is the coolest thing I've ever seen in my life." Despite having her interest piqued again to play the drums, Barbero resisted the urge for another five years.

In the meantime, Lori was earning her title as the Ambassador of the Minneapolis music scene as bands from around the country would perform at First Avenue or 7th Street Entry. When these bands came into town, it was common to see Lori at one of their shows. When the bands got done playing and they needed somewhere to go after the gig, a frequent destination was Lori's house for a party with all her friends who were fans of the band and its crew.

One of the great things about Lori is her modesty and her matter of fact manner that obviously set well with all the bands that became as big a fan of Lori as she was of them. She loved these bands, but she didn't treat them like a crazy fan would. These bands were her friends. The list of bands that have crashed at Lori's house while they were in town is a who's who of the alternative and Seattle music scene. Nirvana, Courtney Love, Dinosaur, Soundgarden, REM, Afghan Wigs, Minutemen, Black Flag, Siouxie and the Banshees to name just a few. For fans of all these bands, the access and closeness that Lori shares with these bands is something they would trade almost anything to experience. For Lori, it seems to get down to a very basic principle.

"I was just a really huge fan," says Barbero. "Even when some of the bands that crashed in my house a few years ago were staying in five-star hotels when they came back in town, they would always come back and spend some time at my place."

When another person would make a statement like that, the first impression may be that they're boasting or rubbing your nose in the fact that she knows them and you don't. With Lori, it never comes across like that. I'm sure if she had an ounce of unscrupulous motives, she has enough dirt on some of the people she knows in the business to write a book or screenplay and make millions. Lori would never do that. That's one of the many reasons why when members from all these bands hear Minneapolis brought up in a conversation from wherever they may be in the world, it's safe to assume that the image of Lori Barbero pops in their head.

When Lori was twenty-six, she finally realized her life-long ambition to become a drummer. The band that she played a role in forming was Babes in Toyland. Lori will be the first one to admit that her drumming skills were extremely limited at the time, but that didn't prevent her from getting the job done.

"I'm a hard working son of a gun. I loved being a drummer," she says. "I had no inkling to play guitar or anything else. I'm just a drummer. We practiced a lot. Eventually, one of our first shows was at 7th Street Entry with a group called Dinosaur, which eventually became Dinosaur Jr. At the time, they were a huge band in the underground scene."

Things happened pretty quickly for Babes in Toyland. "Our first mini-tour was a Midwestern tour with White Zombie," recalls Barbero. "Eventually other bands were asking us to go on tour with them. I'm just a traveler anyway, so living out of a suitcase didn't bother me."

So, Babes in Toyland hit the ground running across the country and soon in Europe.

"Our first time in Europe was with Sonic Youth. That was a huge break. They were the underground icons, still one of my favorite bands. I respect everything they've ever done. They were a big help to us when we started," says Barbero. The festival that Babes in Toyland shared with Sonic Youth in England was the prestigious Reading Festival, a huge break for a relatively new band out of Minneapolis. Babes in Toyland was unique in the genre for the obvious fact that Babes in Toyland was an all woman band. That may have been an initial hook for some people, but the band still had to prove it could deliver. It was obvious to everyone that Babes in Toyland could deliver. What may not have been clear to Lori or the rest of the band was the magnitude of the musical statement they were making.

Now that Lori was not only a fan of the bands but actually one of the bands on tour, her brand of outreach to other musicians became even more immediate and equally as magnetic. One of Lori's closest friendships was with the late Kurt Cobain. As all of us know now, Kurt, Krist, and Dave of Nirvana changed the face of rock and roll. When Lori met the guys, they were just another traveling band. But Lori could tell back then that there was something really special about this particular group.

"There were some guys I met during that time that I knew were going to do better than others," says Barbero. "When Kurt gave me the demo tape for 'Nevermind,' I was living in London. Kurt actually gave it to me. I played it over and over and over, I couldn't even take it out of my tape player. I told Kurt, I told all of them that this was going to be huge, this is so huge I can't believe it. They were like, 'yeah yeah,' they kind of dismissed it. I said, 'no, you don't understand, this is going to be huge, I know it.'"

As Babes in Toyland increased its audience in the U. S. A .and the world, a large portion of the daily grind was on Lori's shoulders. "I was the road manager, I collected all the money, made all the phone calls, I drove the van, checked all of us into the hotels, woke up everybody in the morning to stay on schedule, just basically doing everything," says Lori. "I had no regrets doing it, it was fine and dandy with me." That type of control extended in to all of the Babes in Toyland creative decisions.

Through their negotiations with their eventual major label, Warner Brothers, Lori, the rest of their band and their lawyer insisted on maintaining control of the Babes' images on video and other aspects. They decided who would tour with them, not an A & R person choosing one of their other bands to tour with them. For Lori, it was all about the friendships. If she wasn't confident that the band they were touring with would be compatible, that band wasn't coming on tour. If the record company wanted someone from L. A. or New York City to direct a video or do a photo shoot and someone Lori liked from Minneapolis could do the same thing for far less money, Lori went with the local guys. Babes in Toyland didn't like to be told what to do. That's one of the reasons their fan base was so loyal to them and why Lori was held in such high regard.

From the Reading Festival to Lollapalooza, to being the subject of a book titled "Babes in Toyland—The Making and Selling of a Rock-and-Roll Band," penned by Neal Karlen, to the hundreds of outdoor and club shows that Babes in Toyland played around the world, the girl from south Minneapolis, who played air drums to an Alice Cooper song in fifth grade, certainly came a long way. While it's true that Babes in Toyland wasn't a multi-million-selling group, the impression the band made for music in the '90s and beyond in the alternative scene is undeniable.

"Sometimes people will say things to me like, 'Oh my god you changed my life' and stuff like that," says Barbero. "I'm not very good at compliments, but I do like to hear stuff like that. I'm glad we could have even affected one person to make their lives better, or at least show them something different. To me, that's worth it. I didn't really do it for anyone else. I just did it because it was really really fun."

Currently, Lori Barbero is still heavily involved in the Minneapolis music scene. Her friends from the '80s are still her friends in 2005. Music still thrills her. She rehearses hard multiple times a week with her new band, Koala. She still has very strong commentary on the future of the business and ideas on how to improve it.

"The major record labels are going to go out of business," says Barbero. "Bands are going to do everything on their own and sell their stuff online. Eighty percent of the people in the music business have never picked up a guitar or played live. How could they understand what a band goes through? It should be a prerequisite for working in the music industry to go on the road for a year with a band, or you have to be in a band."

That sounds like a great idea, but both Lori and I know that will never happen. It's all right to dream sometimes.

She is one of the leading MCs and DJs in the Twin Cities. Her presence is still felt at her favorite club, First Avenue in Minneapolis. My daughter Mikaela will testify that Lori's photo album, filled with photos of her with Nirvana, Dave Grohl, Courtney Love, Brad Pitt, Kevin Spacey, and hundreds of other celebs, is the coolest photo album she's ever seen. I'd have to agree with her. Lori made friends around the world. Her music thrills kids now like Alice Cooper thrilled her back in fifth grade. How Lori decides what her next project or effort will be is completely under the control of Lori Barbero. That's as it should be.

When I started playing live in the local clubs of the Twin Cities, the band that ruled was The Lamont Cranston Band. As someone just starting out, to reach the level Lamont Cranston has reached seemed unreachable. Every night they played, they sold the club out. They had released records. They were the model that Dan Ackroyd and John Belushi based the band on that played in *The Blues Brothers* film. They had the opportunity to play in front of the Rolling Stones for a few dates in the Midwest. Everybody knew Lamont Cranston. They were quite simply, the biggest band in town. I wanted to reach that level. I was a long time away from that. Quite honestly, I never reached it. As far as I can tell, nobody but Lamont Cranston has reached that level in the context of the Twin Cities bar circuit better than the Lamont Cranston Band.

Pat Hayes is the face of the Lamont Cranston Band. His name is not Lamont Cranston. His signature sound on the harmonica is instantly recognizable. For more than thirty years The Lamont Cranston Band has carried the torch as they honor the true innovators of the blues. Their dominance in the Twin Cities since then has spawned a lot of Lamont Cranston wannabes. Nobody has reached the level of notoriety and done more for the validity of the Twin Cities bar scene more than Pat Hayes and The Lamont Cranston Band. For Hayes, his role in the current Twin Cities scene is clear. "My bag is the classic blues," says Hayes. "I'm a classical musician of this genre. The pillars of the blues, Howlin' Wolf, Sonny Boy Williamson, Muddy Waters, Little Walter, those are some of the main guys. They were all individual characters and nobody was like them. They were the pillars, everybody followed them."

Pat Hayes is truly carrying the torch for his musical heroes. Although he doesn't fit the standard definition of a classical musician, Hayes feels his contribution to the blues equates with what classical musicians do. "There's two ways of looking at it," he says. "The people in the orchestra play music that's hundreds

It puts hair on your chest

of years old. Just like a classical musician or realistic artist does realistic paintings, performing the songs I perform validate the style. One of the reasons I play what I play is I like the longevity of the style, similar to what classical musicians do."

His commitment to carry the torch for the blues is also based on the tried and true feedback of being able to look at yourself in the mirror every morning. "If I tried to do something that was current to make a buck, first of all, I'd look like an idiot. Second of all, I wouldn't last too long," declares Hayes. The induction of Pat Hayes in to the world of blues and rock and roll began in 1958 when he heard the Fats Domino song, "I'm Gonna Be a Wheel Someday" and Little Richard's "Keep a Knocking But You Can't Come In." "I heard those songs on the radio channel and they just blew me away," recalls Hayes.

Raised in Hamel, a tiny hamlet west of Minneapolis, Hayes' first effort at performing was with a band called the Moon. "The Moon was a psychedelic band," says Hayes. "We were Stones and Yardbirds fans. We would jam for a half an hour on the song 'I'm a Man.' We were freaky. We were an acid rock band influenced by blues styles. When we played we had one strobe light. We were playing keggers and basement parties in the western suburbs. We never got hired for a commercial gig. We were too weird, too far out. Eventually though, that band found out where the music we were playing really came from. It was blues music. As with any band, there's always an evolution that happens the longer you play."

The evolution of Pat Hayes and his band the Moon found themselves digging deeper in to the "pillars" of the blues. "I had a friend who monkeyed around on a harmonica. My brother, Larry, said that Mick Jagger plays the harmonica and the guy from the Yardbirds does too, so I picked it up," says Hayes. "Then I heard Paul Butterfield and said 'Wow, what's that?' I didn't realize it was electric. Right after that, a friend and I went to this record store on 7th and Hennepin in downtown Minneapolis and found a Howlin' Wolf record. My friend bought it but gave it to me later because he didn't like it. When I started listening to it, I realized that this was the same music the Stones and Yardbirds were playing. Then I realized we were getting this kind of music secondhand. The black people were the guys who were doing it right. I was sixteen at the time."

After this revelation, Pat found himself in a group of twelve guys that would start experimenting and discovering their sound, based on these blues giants. "There were about twelve of us that were into the blues," recalls Hayes. "There was a guy we all knew whose parents worked until four in the morning. So nearly every night, all of us would hang out at Wayzata Park, just a bunch of longhairs being looked down upon by the community. Around seven each night, we'd all get in some cars and drive over to this house. We'd rehearse 'til three in the morning. What I remember most was the jamming that would happen in that house. Nobody wanted to be the singer, so I wound up being the singer. Lots of guitars. We actually had enough guys for two bands. One group of those guys became the Lake Street Stink Band, which later became a band called Live Bait. The other group of guys became the first version of The Lamont Cranston Band.

The discovery cycle of Pat Hayes found him juggling a self-admittedly homeless hippie life between the town of Hamel and the West Bank of Minneapolis. "My first gig that paid me money was when I played harmonica at the Coffee House Extempore in the West Bank," recalls Hayes. "I was in a thing called a jug band. It was a community thing, about twenty-five hippies playing guitar and hitting things. That was such a different time. It was organic. It was the West Bank during the Summer of Love."

It puts hair on your chest

Hayes eventually found himself living in a house that featured many members of a band called TBI. One particular night in this house exemplified the musicality of the era. "I went to this big concert during the Aquatennial in 1967 that featured Jefferson Airplane, Buffalo Springfield, and some other bands," recalls Hayes. "The whole place was a swirling mass of lights, lots of incense and stuff. I met this girl at the concert and brought her back to my place where I was living on the porch. As we walked to the house, we could hear the band jamming. For some reason, they sounded really good, better than usual. I go to the door and I see that members of Jefferson Airplane are jamming with TBI. The whole place is packed like sardines. I walk into the kitchen and there's Stephen Stills, David Crosby, and Neil Young. They weren't huge yet, but they still had hits. That's the kind of environment it was back then."

The foundation to the creation of the Lamont Cranston Band had been set through the musical experiences Pat Hayes had as a teenager. The concept of the original Cranston band was to learn from the blues classics and legends and put their own stamp on it. "We were patterning ourselves off the Stones, the Yardbirds, Paul Butterfield, stuff like that," says Hayes. "When we started out playing and recording, we were basically a bluesy swing band. From our first record, we included original material. Back in those days, hardly anybody was recording. In the early- to mid-'60s, there were a whole lot of groups recording at that time in Minnesota. Groups like the Trashmen with 'Surfin Bird,' The Castaways with 'Liar Liar,' and other local bands. When we started recording, it wasn't even really our idea. Some guy with money suggested we record. It never dawned on us to record."

As the Lamont Cranston Band gained popularity, the band's signature sound was starting to be molded. The combination of the harmonica and vocal work of Pat Hayes, the guitar work of Charlie Bingham, and the song writing and vocals of Bruce McCabe proved to be very popular. The strength of these individuals played a huge role in their popularity. As time went on, Pat, Charlie, and Bruce started finding their own voices. When that starts happening, things change. The style of the band would adjust depending on who wrote the song.

"I was still basically a blues and R & B guy," says Hayes. "My bag wasn't really the rock bag. But we were so popular doing it, so I compromised a bit and stayed with it. I always think that there's what you do here, and what you really want to do is over here. You try to keep the two things as close as you can. When it gets too far apart, that's when things can start turning."

Despite some song writing and direction issues within the band, the response from the Twin Cities and the Midwest continued to be huge.

"We probably ruled the roost for more years than anybody in this town, from 1973 to 1983," says Hayes. At the height of the popularity of the band, Lamont Cranston announced to the Twin Cities that they were calling it quits. This was huge news within the music community back then. Cher, The Eagles, and other bands doing a farewell tour were twenty years behind the concept of the long drawn-out farewell tour concept. "That wasn't my idea, it was more of our agent's idea," admitted Hayes. The farewell tour for Lamont Cranston lasted nearly a year, culminating in multiple shows at the Prom Center in St. Paul. While it was a "big scandal at the time," said Hayes, what was clear was that the band was leaving the scene on top. As a fledgling singer in town, I really respected their decision to leave on top.

Without Lamont Cranston, Pat Hayes found himself available to return to his deeper blues roots. His method to show people he was committed to these roots was in the form of his band called Blue Shadows. Part of the reason Pat formed the

It puts hair on your chest

band was to answer some of his critics that thought he sold out and didn't play the real blues anymore, or didn't play the harmonica like Little Walter and a thousand other reasons music snobs criticize anybody who is successful in a blended way that Lamont Cranston achieved. What Pat soon found out was that even though he was eager to show people his real roots, his audience was not ready for Pat to change. His audience wanted Lamont Cranston, not Blue Shadows. Financially, that fact was proven every night he got paid doing Blue Shadows. Conceptually, the people who grew up with Pat Hayes in Lamont Cranston didn't like the change. "Some people would come up to me during the Blue Shadows shows and say, 'Hey Lamont!' and I'd say no, this was Blue Shadows and then they'd say, 'No, you're Lamont! Now play 'Shakedown!'" recalls Hayes.

This type of reaction from his audience and the lukewarm response the other members of his band were receiving with their own projects after the breakup, led them to do a reunion show a year later.

"We did our reunion gig at the Carlton Celebrity Room. It went so well we started thinking we should put the band together again," says Hayes. "We were all floundering. The band was such a force. We actually did put it back together for a year, but the same issues were showing up. The main problems were that none of us were musically happy with what we were doing, we were being compromised."

One project outside of Lamont Cranston that was doing extremely well was a band that Bruce McCabe and Charlie Bingham led, called the Hoopsnakes. The success of this project was evident to Hayes.

"One night Bruce was with the Hoopsnakes at the 5 Corners Saloon," recalls Hayes. "Some guy came up to Bruce and said, 'You look just like the guy that plays piano with The Lamont Cranston Band, but you're better.' I think reactions like that was a big reason Bruce went off to do The Hoopsnakes."

What was also happening with Bruce and Charlie was that they were receiving the adulation that was formerly more focused on Pat when he was the leader of Lamont Cranston. "Charlie and Bruce were getting the pats on the back," says Hayes. "The Hoopsnakes now were the band that ruled the roost, and I was floundering in Palookaville. It was painful for me to see that at the time." The Hoopsnakes did rule the roost for many years, almost as long as Lamont Cranston.

In time, the Hoopsnakes, at least from the outside, seemed to deal with some of the same issues that ended the reign of the Lamont Cranston Band. Bruce McCabe's song-writing skills were becoming in demand for other artists, namely Jonny Lang. The Bruce McCabe song, "Lie to Me" became Jonny Lang's signature song and his first hit. McCabe eventually left the Hoopsnakes to pursue his song writing and to be a key member in Jonny Lang's band that toured as opening acts for the Rolling Stones and Aerosmith, as well as being headliners themselves. Artists have a way of evolving. McCabe was evolving and so was Pat Hayes. After a short time, Pat did resurrect the Lamont Cranston Band at the same time The Hoopsnakes were an extremely hot act in the Twin Cities. Within a short period of time, Hayes discovered that a whole new set of ears—younger ears—were finding out about Lamont Cranston. This new version of Lamont Cranston continued to play clubs around the Twin Cities and the Midwest. They also recorded an original CD called *Roll with Me,* featuring songs that Hayes wrote and produced.

From the mid '80s to today, the Lamont Cranston Band, led by Pat Hayes, is still a leading voice. The band's shows are still well attended. Their reputation is beyond reproach. The respect that Pat Hayes has from musicians around the Twin Cities and the country is stellar. When you've performed for as

It puts hair on your chest

long as Pat Hayes has, there are certain things that drive and guide you to get through another day. There are also some things that you have to come to grips with. One of those things is being known as Lamont Cranston. "When I started Blue Shadows I didn't want to be Lamont, in fact I never was Lamont," says Hayes. "But I realize I can't not be Lamont. I am Lamont. I have to live with it whether I like it or not."

Concerning Lamont Cranston, Pat is philosophical about people's views on his career. "It's always the first version that sticks in people's minds, you got to live with that," says Hayes. "Popularity comes and goes and there's not much you can do about it. If you're an artist, you just continue to work. A real artist goes on and on whether anybody likes it or not. That's what separates the real musicians from the phonies. Ones that stop playing because they didn't get their record deal, fame, or money, they drop by the wayside. Dylan and the Stones look to the likes of Willie Dixon and Howlin' Wolf and Willie Nelson as their models. I look to people like Dave Ray, Bob Dylan, and the Stones as my model." Pat Hayes is very happy with his slot in the Twin Cities music scene. He also understands that his profession is something that everybody just won't understand.

"It's almost impossible for anybody to understand what it is to be a musician," says Hayes. "Because the whole thing is based on projection. As an artist, you should always be looking six months ahead, and the dream is always in the back of your mind. You're the only one who sees it, though. Other people can't. Artists are driven by the intangible. If you're driven by money, people can see it. If you're an artist, people don't exactly know what's driving you. They just have to wait until you finish your project and that's the mystery. That's what keeps it exciting."

In St. Paul, there's a club called the Minnesota Music Cafe. One of the owners is Billy Larson, leader of a legendary Twin

Cities band called Raggs. Billy and his business partner, Karen Palm, are celebrating their seventh year of existence. On the walls of the performance area inside the club hang multiple banners of Twin Cities musicians who've made an impact. The names range from international stars like Prince, Dylan, the Time, and the Replacements to established Twin Cities legends like Eddie Berger, Big Walter Smith, Lamont Cranston, the Metro All-Stars, Raggs, and Debbie Duncan, along with present day popular bands like G. B. Leighton, Soul Tight Committee, and thankfully, Mick Sterling and the Stud Brothers. The walls of the Minnesota Music Cafe are a reflection of the importance of the live music scene and how it helps mold the tone and scope of a city. The concept of the Minnesota Music Cafe honors the past and provides the present lovers of local music the combination of a great showcase stage, hearty bar food, and a good drink as they honor the past musicians and encourage present day and future musicians.

As many names that are on these walls, there are hundreds of equally worthy names who didn't make the wall. There are thousands of stories that should be told to many, but will most likely remain within the confines of the band in which the stories came from. What all of us in the Twin Cities music community share is the ability to share our gift. The validity of the gift is subjective depending on who is listening to it and personal tastes. The gift the club-goer hears live or on a recording comes from someone or something that influenced your favorite artist. The gift you hear was handed down from another source. That concept will always remain true.

"If you can go out and entertain people," says Hayes, "that's a real blessing. It's a gift from God and it's your responsibility to use that gift." I'm glad I have the ability to share that gift with whoever wants to hear it.

It puts hair on your chest

This was taken at the Tap Room in Duluth in March 2005. Duluth holds a special place in my heart. They really seem to get the band up there. They have been very supportive of what I'm trying to do. The fact that people make the effort to come and see us, despite the thousand other things they could be doing, is something that always amazes me. (Photo Credit: Daniel Schilles)

Could you sign this for my friend?

Chapter 9

I **was watching "The Tonight Show with Jay Leno."** This was during the tragedy of the tsunami flooding in Sri Lanka, Indonesia, and other Asian islands. On this particular show, Jay was encouraging all the guests to sign a beautiful Harley-Davidson motorcycle parked near Jay's desk on the set. The result of all the signatures on the Harley would be that *The Tonight Show* would offer it on eBay, with the money from the highest bidder going to a charity to help the victims. It's cool that Jay does this. He seems like a very generous and hard-working fellow. He has the number-one late night show. He's got the bully pulpit to get something like this done. Each celebrity he interviewed grabbed the best little friend a celebrity has— the black Sharpie pen—and walked over and signed the bike. That's beautiful stuff. If a celebrity signature will increase the bid on the bike, all the better. It seems so perfect, so why does it bother me?

On the show that night was Dustin Hoffman. I love Dustin Hoffman. I even loved him in *Ishtar*. The crowd gave him a standing ovation. They loved that he would get in his car and drive to the studio just to take time out of his busy life to pick up a black Sharpie pen and sign a motorcycle. The crowd treated this activity by Dustin

Hoffman as if it was a very difficult and selfless thing to do. When in actuality, his publicist loved it because he's being seen as compassionate. The film company that produced *Meet the Fockers* loved it because it increased the chances that a family of four with two kids under the age of twelve will blow $100 exposing their kids to inappropriate humor for children. The end result leaving the parents broke at the end of the night and the little kids with nightmares and questions because they saw Barbara Streisand and Dustin Hoffman touching each other. Old people touching each other. Yuck.

Now there's a very real possibility that Dustin Hoffman did this purely because he wanted to help. I'm sure he did. He's been in enough films. He doesn't need the publicity or recognition. If he just would have signed the motorcycle off the air, or before the show, wouldn't the bike get as much money on eBay? What bothers me is P. R. people and the descendants of *The Arsenio Hall Show* audience shouting, screaming, and applauding at meager comedic, dramatic, and compassionate moments. The people were freaking out because Dustin Hoffman signed a motorcycle. Some things don't require applause just because the sign tells you to do it.

As a local singer who's released his own CDs for many years, the concept of the autograph has always intrigued me. The fact that some people perceive the actual process of giving an autograph to be such an imposition for the signer is peculiar. How long people wait for autographs amazes me. What is the payoff for someone who receives the autograph? How does it feel after you get an autograph? Does having the autograph make you listen to the CD or read the book more intently? As someone who's never asked for anybody's autograph, the fascination of receiving an autograph is interesting to me. As someone who's asked to give autographs, I'm just grateful people even know who I am.

Lets clear something up right now. Giving an autograph is not an exhausting procedure. When someone gives you an autograph, they haven't done an extraordinarily difficult thing. The fact that a fan takes time out of their busy life to walk over to you, or wait in line to get your autograph, is something not to be treated lightly. It's an extraordinary thing to sign an autograph. The fact that it means so much to get your signature on something means something. However, like with all things, sometimes the pursuit of an autograph can get a bit dicey. Lots of planning and scheming can take place to get an autograph. Sometimes all that preparation can get a select few in a lather and they do something weird. It's a shame when a writing tool so pure and beautiful as the black Sharpie pen is being used for ulterior motives. The placement of an autograph can at times be interesting. The vast majority of people who want autographs want their books, photos, CDs, or posters signed. Sometimes people want their arm signed, occasionally a bald head or their hand. These autographs go home with them and they get placed on the wall or in a scrapbook or, if it's on a body part, stared at in the mirror, I suppose. I love signing autographs. I'm happy to do it. Except when I get the request to put the pen near a hot spot. When women want me to autograph a particular erogenous zone, that's when I start putting the cap back on the Sharpie.

The signature on breasts, thighs, and asses are ones that puzzle me to this day. What do you do with those autographs? Do you not wash them off for days? Do you show your spouse or significant other that you took time out of your day to have a relative stranger put a pen in a place where your lover's hands were last night? I always picture the reaction of my wife if she saw me with my hands between a woman's legs signing an autograph, or witnessing me while I put my name on a breast. She wouldn't like that. It would make her feel bad and hurt her

Could you sign this for my friend?

feelings. I don't want that. I know if I saw my wife doing that, I would have some manhood issues to deal with at a bare minimum. Thankfully, I don't think the roles are reversed very often. I don't think that men wait in line to have their johnson's signed. At least I hope they don't. Honestly, it's not very pretty down there. Frankly, I don't know why women are attracted to our junk in the first place. If you've ever been in a men's locker room at a fitness club, you'd understand my view.

Some musicians dig signing their name anywhere a woman asks them to. They think it's kind of a joke. I see the humor in it too, just not as much as others do. Maybe it's because I have always been surrounded by women in my life. Signing autographs on particular parts of a woman's body is something I just don't do. It's just isn't me. It's been done. Maybe if they asked me to sign their spleen, that might pique my curiosity.

Then there are the times when women want me to sign something on their CD or picture that declare once and for all the level of my lust toward the recipient of the autograph. This can take the form of me signing that I "love" that person, or I want to have sex with this person, something along those lines. I don't do that stuff either.

I firmly believe that whatever you write, even if it's meant to be humorous, can be misconstrued by someone. It also has a very real possibility of lingering in the shadows and rearing its ugly head at the worst times. I don't need a woman I never met showing a statement to everybody about a sexual romp that I never had—or would ever have—in a million years. That's why when I'm asked to sign something stating how I "have to have" a woman, I just sign my name, and shake my head. If they become upset, I'm confident they'll forget about it in the morning.

Sometimes the autograph you sign is for someone else. If the person asking for an autograph is embarrassed about having their own name, they'll make up another person to have you sign it for. It's like telling a story to someone about the troubles your "friend" is having when the story is about yourself. I always think if you're embarrassed to admit that you want the autograph, why get the autograph at all? I can see being intimidated to ask for an autograph from Brad Pitt or George Clooney. At least your momentary embarrassment may pay off someday and you're friends will think it's cool. But I'm just a townie, why be intimidated by me? I'm just a local guy who can sing in pitch most of the time. Nevertheless, I'll sign something if someone wants it.

If my autograph actually is for someone else, did that person who is receiving the autograph actually want it in the first place? Do they even know who the hell I am? Most times, I think not. While it's not a necessity for me to actually know the person I'm signing the autograph for, it's always struck me funny as to why someone would wait in line for me to sign an autograph for someone else. I'm happy to sign it, just a little suspect of the motive, that's all.

In a perfect and just world, the people who should be giving autographs are fireman, teachers, policeman, surgeons, doctors, nurses, troops who are protecting our country, and all the other professions where your knowledge really makes a difference in the world. But we all know they rarely get asked. The majority of the time, the people with these kinds of jobs are taken for granted by all of us. They do it so well and they help so many people so regularly, that we don't deem it worthy of an autograph. Instead, some people have a tendency to want autographs from the likes of Kato Kaelin, Scott Peterson, and Robert Blake, just because they've been in the news. Even prisoners on death row have people out there who would accept their autograph, just to say they have it. To state my position clearly, I'm not equating the people who want my autograph to people who want autographs from prisoners on death row. It's just an extreme example of how far people will go to have any kind of connection with someone doing something out of the norm.

In the Scorcese film *The King of Comedy* with Robert DeNiro and Jerry Lewis (on an off note, Jerry Lewis was brilliant in this film), DeNiro spends his days and nights lumped in a group of star seekers, just aching for the opportunity to get close to a star. If they can't have a relationship with them, an autograph will do the trick. He shows off his autographs to the other hunters in the pack. Eventually, getting an autograph isn't cutting it anymore. He wants to be Jerry Langford, the character that Jerry Lewis portrayed, who was the king of late-night television. It's one of my favorite DeNiro films. It's filled with dark humor, but at its core it's a sad tale. Thankfully, I'm sure the people who want my autograph aren't sad or psychotic. Hopefully they were inspired by what I recorded or just witnessed in a live setting to want my autograph. People want to be connected somehow to someone outside of their everyday world. There's nothing wrong with that if the expectation is rational.

Since we're not robots, signing an autograph is not solely based on signing. For me, it usually means a short conversation, a handshake, a hug, or a kiss on the cheek. Sometimes you hear deeply personal stories from someone based on some personal moment that I played an important role in. I love those moments. I love the fact that my music or my performance meant so much to someone that they felt the need to communicate it to me. They waited for me to tell me something, the least I can do is listen to them and hopefully make the moment something they'll remember.

Any musician who refuses to sign an autograph is too jaded and should be out of the business as far as I'm concerned. You might as well stay in your basement and record those songs that no one but your pot-smoking high-school friends will understand. The ego involved to refuse to sign an autograph is bordering on pathetic. It takes ten seconds of your life. You can still be a jerk, just sign it, walk away, and don't even look at the person who wants the autograph if that makes it easier. Those are the kinds of musicians who need angst and turmoil in their life so they make the act of signing an autograph a torturous ordeal. Grow up and sign it. Is that so hard?

Every time I sign an autograph, I realize the courage it took for someone to ask me. I appreciate the opportunity I have and the responsibility I possess to make that make that moment mean something. I realize I'm a local singer and I may be signing these autographs at a town fair or a tiny club. It doesn't really matter where I sign it, the principle is still the same. A profession you spent years of hard work crafting has moved someone to ask for something as personal as how you sign your name. It's a small gesture that means a lot to someone. Plus, it's just cool that someone wants my autograph. Isn't that one of the reasons we started playing an instrument or start singing in the first place? Musicians need to remember that sometimes.

Could you sign this for my friend?

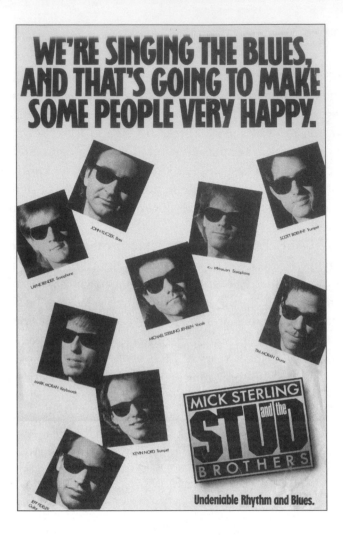

This is the first poster I saw at the first rehearsal of The Stud Brothers in Mark and Tim Moran's basement. Tim designed it. The faces weren't on it yet, but the layout was the same. I loved the pitch, and the name of the band made me laugh. It was a name that you wouldn't forget once you heard it. This was an exciting time for me. Lots of rehearsals, lots of laughs, zero money, but we got to play Tower of Power, Otis, James Brown, and Wilson Pickett songs. Nothing wrong with that.
(The original band: Top four, from left to right—Layne Bender—Sax, John Kuczek—Bass, Jeff Fawbush—Sax, Scott Bohne—Trumpet; Middle—Me; Bottom four, from left to right—Mark Moran—Hammond Organ, Tim Moran—Drums, Kevin Nord—Trumpet, Jeff Fideler—Guitar)

Who's responsible?

Chapter 10

Whenever a performance or project is perceived as flawless, the most logical perception would be that the effort to produce it was easy. Every topic has a variety of options to explore before the final resolution. Opinions fly off our tongues fast and furiously. Sometimes we actually expect what we say to contribute and solve something, we just say things to hear ourselves speak. What you don't see, (or should see, you've got better things to do with your day) is the spark it took to create the idea that created the project or product. You don't see the compromises and creativity it took to find the right combination of people and skills to have it come to fruition. You don't see the mistakes and second-guessing that ultimately happens within any project. You don't see the twists and curves it took from the original idea to the final product. You don't see the backbiting and suspicions of a few select people who seem to find countless ways of intentionally or unintentionally tripping you up. You don't see the people who, once they've been hired to do a project, baffle you with their apathy and pace when you're trying to get something done. You don't see the seemingly endless conversations with your clients about anything except the reason the relationship was started in the first place. Such is the blessing and the curse of being a leader in the business or political world. The music business is no different, no matter what level you're at.

When someone is watching a band, it's natural to assume things. Some of these assumptions are based on stereotypes and some are based on what's in front of them. You can easily assume that someone who's outrageous on stage would have to be the same off stage. You can think that all the band members on stage are using some form of a drug. You can think that all of the band members cheat on their girlfriends or wives—or boyfriends and husbands—at will. The actual word for the main content of a musician's career is the biggest assumption non-musicians make. People work. Musicians play. The word *play* creates the image to people that musicians aren't actually working. It's not their real job. They can't be making a living doing what they do. Unfortunately, the latter point is more than often true.

It's tough to make a living depending solely on playing live in club land. The Twin Cities music scene is stronger than most, but the fact is money is still tough out there. What is misguided is the perception that musicians aren't really working when they're performing. Certainly it's a unique job, but it's a job nonetheless. The basic framework of that job, and every job out there, is the same. Someone had to create it. Someone has to have the final say on how that job happens. Someone has to be the boss, whether that person wants the job or not. I've been very fortunate to avoid a common pitfall that plays a big role in the breakup of bands: the element of jealousy and envy of one member of the band being noticed more than someone else.

Even when I wasn't the official leader of a band I was in, the fact that I was the lead singer made me the leader in the eyes of the people watching the band. I sing the songs. I talk to the crowd. I'm the closest to the audience. In the club-goers' eyes, that makes me the leader of the band. When I watch a band, my natural assumption would be that the person who's out front is the leader. The front person may not be the behind-the-scenes leader, but on stage (that's the only place as a fan I could see the band) the front person is perceived as the leader. Since I became a band leader, the members of my band have understood what role I have to play and the role they play. Neither one is more important than the other. Each member plays an important role in creating our sound. But some things are just plain common sense. You can't have everyone in the group trying to be the front person. There has to be a foundation built— the kick drum, the bass, the groove, the chords, the melody, and other ingredients. The natural person to lead the performance side of the group is the front person. The best way to keep a band together is to find a group of musicians who understand that dynamic.

Not everyone is built to be a band leader. Many musicians wouldn't want the job in the first place. They like to remain in a group setting that limits their responsibility to the gig to the mere fact of showing up on time for gigs and rehearsals. As a band leader, having a band that shows up on time for gigs and rehearsals is fantastic. But it takes more to keep the gig than just showing up on time. Much more.

There are few things that are certain in the music business. Two that I know are: I've never heard of a black singer wanting to sing like a white singer, and the other is whoever controls the money is held suspect at some level by band members.

The path the money takes from the client can travel through multiple filters before anybody in the band sees a check. In the local scene, the most common path is this: the club pays the leader, the leader pays the agent, the leader pays him or herself, and then the leader pays the band. The method, the accuracy, and the timing of these payments are critical to the success or failure of all bands. In order for any live band to get paid, they have to find a gig. For many bands, the persons who find those gigs are agents. Oh those wonderful agents!

I have to admit, my experiences with agents have for the most part been terrific. When I first started playing in the '80s, I was in a band that relied on an agent to get gigs. It was a benchmark for us at the time to find an agency that actually had enough faith in our talent to think they could make money off of us. We were with a Minnesota-based agency called Variety Artists. We were young and very green while we were dealing with them. The agency would get us gigs in the Twin Cities and in smaller towns in Minnesota and Wisconsin.

To keep our end of the deal, we purchased a school bus, took out all the seats so we could put all of our sound gear, lights, and instruments in the back while we traveled. We were exclusive with Variety Artists. That meant we couldn't find any gigs on our own; they had to come from the agency. That was fine with us. We didn't know other club owners as well as they did. Plus, we dug the fact that someone was making calls on our behalf. Of course, once the agent makes the calls and we agree to the gig, we have to make sure we get to the gig and satisfy the club. That happened occasionally. What happened more often than not was that the club just didn't get what we were doing. What was also happening was that it was harder for us to get to gigs that were farther out of town than we wanted to travel. Plus, the money we were getting was very low because we were a relatively new band. Paying an agent 15 percent, leaving each band member $20 in their pocket after all the rehearsals, the loading and unloading of gear from our practice space, onto the bus, off the bus, into the club, out of the club, back on the bus, and back into the rehearsal space was getting a little old.

When things start getting bad, it's easy to blame the agent. We figured the 15 percent included giving us the option to blame them first when things went wrong. Agents are easy scapegoats when things go wrong. In reality, while agents can be blamed for some things, the majority of issues bands have with gigs and how much they get paid can't be solved by agents. They have to be solved internally. An agent is not your mother. An agent is not your manager. The agent's job is to find you a gig so you get paid and they get paid. That's about it.

My relationship with an exclusive agent ended on a bus ride back from a weekend summer gig we had with this same band in Alexandria, Minnesota. We had just played a Friday night gig that we thought went very well. Lots of people were dancing and drinking. The crowd responded to us pretty well. As we were sitting on the beach, basking in our per-ceived glory in Alexandria the next afternoon, we got a mes-sage that the owner of the club wanted to see us. When we returned the club, they told us that we weren't the band our agent had told them we were. They thought they were getting a band that played classic rock material. We leaned more toward Springsteen, Elvis Costello, and Southside Johnny and the Asbury Jukes. Obviously there was poor communica-tion between our agent and the club. Trouble was brewing.

As we drove home in our vehicular tribute to the Partridge Family bus, the conversation between the band members was heated. In a nutshell, the club owner was an idiot. He didn't know what good music was. The agent was trying to screw us for the 15 percent and, despite what the club owner said, we were still a fan-tastic band. We were fed up. We got fired and everyone and every-thing sucked. We could either try and fix our problems with the agent or ignore our perceived stupidity of the club owner that fired us and move on. Or we could just quit and try and enjoy the rest of our summer. We quit on the bus ride home. We called the agent and said that we quit. We sold the bus. No more problems. You can do that in your late teens and early twenties.

Agents play a key role in the live music scene in any city. The necessity of an agent for the success of your band is in the hands of the leader of the band. The first issue you have to tackle as a band is agreeing on whether you need an agent in the first place.

For as many complaints as I hear about agents from other bands, I often wonder why they decided to be exclusive with an agent in the first place. Agents have phones, faxes, and e-mail. So do bands. Agents use the U. S. mail. So do musicians. Agents have phone books. So do musicians. Why do new bands immediately think an agent is the only person who can get them jobs? While it's harder to get gigs when you start out without an agent, it's not impossible. When a band makes the decision one way or the other, the band has to accept the hardships that go along with their decision. With an agent, you immediately lose 15 percent of whatever you make. If you've signed an exclusive agreement with an agent, you're placing the financial success of your band on one person. You also add the element of staying on top of the agent to make sure you get the right gigs as you progress. You also place an enormous amount of trust in the agent to represent you properly to club owners prior to and after the gig. For all this responsibility, the agent gets 15 percent of what you make.

What so many bands struggle with concerning agents is that the 15 percent they earn seems to come to them with something as simple as a phone call or e-mail. Many agents will book multiple dates with bands in one phone call to the band leader. A common scenario starts with the agent calling the band leader. The agent is offering multiple dates from a specific club to your band. Lets say each offer is for $1,000 per gig and the agent is offering five gigs. You check your schedule. If you're open, you accept the dates. How you look at this transaction is crucial to the success of your band.

When the band gets paid $1,000 for each gig and the club books the band five times within the year, the band has a contractual agreement to be paid $5,000 from one club. The agent has a contractual agreement to be paid $150 per gig from that agreement, making your band pay a total of $750 from one club to your agent. Your band will spend four to six hours at that club per performance for that $5,000. The agent will spend less than one hour between the phone call and the creation of the contracts to mail to the leader for his $750. At first impression, the time discrepancy is huge. Plus, the agent is one person. All the money goes to one person. Like most things, it isn't quite that simple.

That $150 per gig the agent receives is payment for multiple responsibilities beyond the actual phone call. The agent may have a staff and office expenses. The agent may have to do follow-up phone calls for your band. If your band failed in the room or one of the band members acted like a jerk in the club that night, the agent hears about it. If you want to get more money from the club, the agent is your advocate (and his or her own advocate because the more money you make, the more money the agent makes). The agent also has to take the responsibility of finding another group in case your group breaks up and the club is at risk of being without a band because of it. The agent has to make sure that he keeps track of your performance schedule so you're not double booked somewhere. The agent also has to deal with all of the band's questions and concerns about big things like actual gigs to having to solve problems within the band. All of that is why the agent is making $150 on a $1,000 gig. As a band, you have to come to grips with if dealing with all of that is worth $150, or if you want to take on those potential headaches and keep the $150 within the band.

Some headaches are worth getting. If the agent has a lineup of multiple bands that are exclusive with him or her, the agent stands to do very well in club land. If the agent has five bands at five different clubs every Friday or Saturday, that's ten gigs a weekend. If the average commission on those gigs is $150, that's $1,500 per weekend, $6,000 a month. While it's true it takes more than a series of phone calls to book bands, it ain't like working in a coal mine.

Being an agent, while at times can be frustrating and maddening, is potentially a very good gig indeed. As in any business, there are scumbags and there are guys who deliver what they promise. More often than not, agents deliver what they promise. As a band, once you make that decision to use an agent, you have to suck it up and write that check, even if you don't want to do it, no matter what type of person your agent is. Without the agent, you wouldn't have gotten the gig. You may have been able to get the gig on your own, but you didn't want to take that risk or you didn't want that responsibility to find work at that club. Sure you can get the gig now because people know you, but they wouldn't have known about you without the assistance of the agent in the early stages of your band. If the band wants to complain about it, they can do it directly to the agent, or they can hire a manager to yell at the agent. Of course, you do have to pay the manager too, but what is that manager doing for you?

The style of music you perform may dictate the need to become exclusive with an agency, or accept offers from various agents for gigs without the need for exclusivity. The beginning days and the first couple of years of Mick Sterling and the Stud Brothers provided us with a great platform to be able to pick and choose the time and place for the help from agents. We were lucky, but our choices provided that luck.

I had been back for a few months from my two-and-a-half-year stint with a full-time band in St. Louis. I was involved with another band called Blue Heat (eventually called The Nightburners) at the time that was performing covers and original material. We rehearsed a lot but played out rarely. My wife and I had just had our first child, our daughter Mikaela. I was spending four to five days a week, driving thirty-five miles each way to rehearsal each night for little in return. I was happy with the songs we were writing, but after working all day and rehearsing at night, I was barely seeing my wife and my new child. During this time, I received a phone call from Mark Moran, a high school friend and an old band mate of mine. He told me he was putting together a big horn band and he wanted me to be the singer. Since my early days of performing were with Mark in a similar style of band, I was attracted to the concept of it. However, since I'd done these types of bands before, I was hesitant to try and put it together.

It took too long. There was little money in it. Most of all, I was already committed to another band at the time. This band was writing original material and I liked all the guys in the band. But the length of the drive each night and the lack of gigs were really starting to bother me. I told Mark that if he wants to put it together, I'd be happy to sing for it, but I just didn't have the time to find people.

In a few weeks, I got a phone call from Mark telling me that he had put a band together and a rehearsal was scheduled. The rehearsal was in the basement of his parent's house, the place we used to rehearse years ago. I was looking forward to seeing Mark and his brother Tim, and the new guys he chose for this band. As I walked into the garage and through the basement door of Moran's house, the first thing I saw was a poster. On this poster, there were nine black squares placed in various positions with a slogan on top that said: "We're singing the blues, and that's going to make some people very happy." In the bottom right corner of the poster was a logo that said Mick Sterling and the Stud Brothers. I saw the name of the band and I laughed. I loved the poster. I loved the fact that they chose the name of the band before we even had a rehearsal. I loved the fact they just assumed that I was in the band before I had even gone to a rehearsal. From that moment on, I was in the band. From that moment on, despite how many times I corrected people in the first few months of the band—if the band played—they wouldn't know me as Michael Sterling Jensen, they would know me as Mick Sterling. I was in the band.

We rehearsed a bunch of Tower of Power, Otis Redding, Wilson Pickett, and James Brown songs. After being separated from this type of band for a few years, singing these songs again was like wrapping myself in my magic blanket when I was a kid. Musically, it felt like home to me. It was also a lot less pressure for me to rehearse with this band than my other band. There was far less of a time commitment, and the songs were stronger. Plus we had a great horn section. I was in two bands that required my time—time which I didn't have to give. I had to make a choice. Despite how much fun the new band was, I had simply put too much time in the other band to leave it. The Stud Brothers would have to find a new front man. As usual, Kristi persuaded me to not be so hasty. Kristi had a very good feeling about the Stud Brothers. She really didn't want me to leave the band, despite the fact the Stud Brothers were in the same position as my other band: no gigs, which meant no money coming in. After a few more long drives out to the rehearsal space with Blue Heat, Kristi's concerns, and my obvious affection for what the other band was doing, I decided it was in my best interest to leave my first band and focus on the Stud Brothers.

It felt good to make the change. But the main problem was still at hand. Where are the gigs going to come from?

The Stud Brothers' quest for gigs was similar to every new band. We wanted to play on the weekend at the best clubs in the Twin Cities. We had nine guys in the band, which meant that with a soundman, whatever we got paid from the club was going to be split nine ways and the soundman would make far more than we would most of the time. Our search for clubs began. Our response from clubs was the same. Either you play the club for damn near nothing or you won't play the club on a weekend night. Nobody knew who we were, why should they hire us? Our other problem was that even if we got a gig on a weekend night, could we keep the same caliber of players on board to play for $5 or $10 on a weekend night? We found out rather quickly that we couldn't. Even in the beginning, we all knew this band was special, but it became very obvious to everyone that we needed to change our game plan. We simply couldn't keep everyone on board without gigs. A meeting was held at Tim Moran's house. Mark Moran, our guitar player Jeff Fideler, our sax player Layne Bender, and myself were brainstorming, trying to find a way to keep the band together. During our conversation, I brought up something that Kristi had told me happened when we lived in St. Louis that may apply to our situation.

In a northern suburb of St. Louis, there was a little bar off the highway that would have a blues band perform on Sunday afternoons. This band was really nothing to speak of. The musicians were fine but they weren't great. The stuff they were playing was standard blues stuff. What made this situation so remarkable was that this band was playing for a full house on a Sunday afternoon. It may be the most beautiful Sunday afternoon outside, but for some reason people would find their way to this smoky little bar and watch this blues

Who's responsible?

band. It was more than the music. It was the hang. It was the vibe. It was this little secret club that these people had each Sunday. Maybe we could create something like this in Minneapolis.

Doing an every-Sunday gig would solve some problems. The biggest one being that at least on a Sunday, we knew everybody would be off. In 1988, the clubs in Minneapolis on Sunday nights were either closed or had first-time bands. It was basically a dead night in town. Nobody was doing much to speak of. The fact that it was dead also proved that people weren't used to going out on a Sunday night, which could defeat the whole thing right out of the gate. We agreed at the meeting that finding a Sunday night gig was a good thing to try. It was also agreed at that meeting that Bunkers Music Bar and Grill in Minneapolis was the place to do it.

We had played Bunkers a few times before in a previous band called Heat Treatment. We felt comfortable with the place. This was the place. We knew the club wouldn't pay us much for a Sunday night so we decided to take that out of the equation. We made them an offer.

The offer was this: the band will play for six weeks for free, as long as the club puts an ad in the weekly music magazine *City Pages* telling people we were there. If, after six weeks, the club doesn't like the way it's going, the club can let us go. Zero risk, no fee for a nine-piece soul and R & B band. Bunkers decided to go for it. In a couple of Sundays after the proposal, we played our first Sunday night at Bunkers.

Our first few weeks were lightly attended. However, the people who were there were energized by our sound. At that time, there just weren't big horn bands playing. Our approach was more commercial than other blues bands in town, so it was easier to latch on to. After our sixth week, Bunkers decided to keep us on. Each week after that, more people would start checking us out. I remember one week when local blues legend Big Walter Smith was chuckling while my skinny white self sang the song Big Twist and Mellow Fellows made famous, "300 Pounds of Heavenly Joy."

Musicians were coming to check us out. That was cool. But for us, what was more important was that we were starting to get a whole new audience. Hair stylists, waiters, waitresses, bartenders, hotel workers, and other hospitality industry workers were starting to make this an every Sunday thing. Sunday night was their night off; they worked on Friday and Saturday nights. Our Sunday nights at Bunkers were starting to become what happened in that little smoky bar in St. Louis. It was a hang. It was a vibe. It was a secret club. Within a year, our "secret club" was starting to have members who would wait in line on the sidewalk to get in each Sunday. Our Sunday nights were exploding.

Other clubs started to notice. When they asked how to hire us, they were surprised to see we didn't have an agent. We built it on our own, and we booked it on our own.

Within two years, Mick Sterling and the Stud Brothers were playing nearly two hundred times a year. The majority of these gigs were our steady gigs on Sundays and Tuesday nights, (unprecedented at the time) and weekend nights in other clubs. All of our gigs were word-of-mouth. The clients and clubs would come to us. They wanted to capture the vibe that happened at Bunkers in their club. Sometimes it worked, sometimes it didn't. But the machine was rolling. If an agent asked us to play a club, sometimes we'd take it. It would depend on if we liked the club or if the money was right. It was nice to be in the position to choose instead of grasping for anything that came our way. We stuck to a plan and it worked. We took a shot to do things on our own and it paid off.

In order for any band to succeed, it has to have a vision. It has to have someone who leads the way. A band in theory is a democracy but in practice is closer to a dictatorship. If you do it right, it's not a ruthless dictatorship but a dictatorship that is fully granted to the leader and supported due to the way the leader conducts him- or herself. The leader of a band in many ways is in a more tenuous position than an agent in band members' eyes because the band members see the leader of the band at every gig and rehearsal, as opposed to a mainly phone-conversation relationship with an agent.

The leader of the band has to have a relationship with the band members that are based on many things. There are a few ways to lead a band. One way is through intimidation. This kind of leader seems to take some pleasure in keeping all the band members on edge as a constant reminder as to who's the boss. If you're this kind of leader, it would be natural to assume that the leader who leads by intimidation should be a champion in their chosen instrument or vocally. In my experience, that isn't always the case. What this type of leader lacks in depth of talent in their instrument, they make up for in the ability to manipulate circumstances to put them in a position of power over the other band members. This kind of leader is constantly being talked about behind his or her back, but rarely confronted. If you want the gig this leader is on, you do it the way he or she tells you too. If you mess up, you either get fined or you get fired. Both options are usually done quickly and decisively. If the leader is conflicted about it, he or she never shows it. They just find another person to fill the void of your firing and they get the job done.

If you're the person who writes the checks to the band members, you naturally become someone who's treated a bit differently from other band members. Some band members may act a certain way with other band members, but most of the time they won't act that way toward the leader. I'm confident the tenor of the conversation between band members after the gig is modified when the leader is in the mix. It seems like a natural tendency to do this. When someone's the boss, you don't want your boss to know everything.

I've never been one to impose myself as a band leader. I've always had a hard time telling grown men how to conduct themselves. I've been very fortunate to have played with a strong group of professionals who didn't need guidance; they just did their job really well. I have no interest in intimidating or pressuring guys. I have no desire to fine someone if they're late; we don't make enough money in my estimation to merit that. For better or for worse, the caretaker part of my personality normally takes over when I'm in leader mode. I want everyone to feel comfortable and inspired. I don't like conflict. In order to avoid conflict, I will go the extra mile and do everything I can to resolve the issue, even if it's really not my issue to solve. If I have to take some blame to solve it, I'll do it. It's times like this that I wish I had the power of intimidation, but I know I don't.

Whatever type of leader you are, the one thing that's expected of you is to deal with all the bad things that happen within your band. Dealing with agents and club owners. Dealing with band members who aren't working out. If someone needs to be fired, all the complaining from other band members isn't going to get rid of that guy. The leader must make the final decision and go face-to-face and fire that band member. The leader must deal with all the behind-the-scenes drama of the band. The band members go to the leader, sometimes to solve the issue, other times just to vent. Either way, the band leader plays many roles besides what the public sees on stage.

One of the worst things you have to do as a leader is fire someone. In my history as a band leader, I've only had to do this a few times. I'm not good at this. It goes completely against my caretaker mentality. I want to find a way to make things work. But sometimes for the good of the band a change needs to happen. These situations are at times obvious and at other times seem to come from out of the blue to the person being fired. I've fired people over the phone and face-to-face. I've had to fire people primarily one person at a time. There was an occasion when I had to let go of the entire rhythm section. Not because of the ability of any individual member, but it was due to the combination of the members and the sound they were creating. Sometimes combinations just don't work. This one didn't, and I needed to make a change. My future in leading the band was dependent on this decision. I was so unhappy with the sound of the band that I considered quitting myself. That didn't happen. I made the decision to dramatically alter the band for the good of the concept of the Stud Brothers as a whole. This decision led to the main lineup of my band to this day. It was a good decision to make, but it was a tough one. I'm sure the guys who were released didn't think it was, but in my head and my gut I knew had to do it. As a leader, you have to live with your decisions.

As hard as letting someone go is, I've always tried to do it with as much respect as I could. As much as I've tried to do it respectfully, I have made mistakes. My two worst mistakes showcased my lack of discipline and strength at the time.

Back in the early '90s, there was a member of my band who was receiving a lot of criticism from the opinionated members of the band. They wanted him out. What he was playing was not working for them. To make matters worse, we were a few days away from recording a live CD at Bunkers. We had done many rehearsals to get ready to record. These rehearsals and performances were adding fuel to the fire for certain band members to eliminate the band member they perceived as not pulling his weight. As the leader, I had to juggle the feelings of the opinionated members of the band, keep the momentum going so we could record on the scheduled date, and deal with my own feelings about how this person was doing. I struggled with this for many days. In the end, I set a meeting with the band member. During our conversation at a coffee shop one morning, I told him the position of some of the members in the band. It was a situation that could only be solved by letting this member go. It was very, very tough. This band member had kids. He was a great guy. He showed up on time and he never failed to deliver when asked to do something. So why did I feel I needed to fire him?

My reason at the time was that it was for the good of the band. If I fired this person, the main voices in the band would feel better about going into our recording process. It would reinvigorate the band. It may have done that temporarily, but to this day it's always felt like I made the decision far too hastily. My gut was telling me this band member didn't deserve to be fired, but despite how I felt, I did. As a band leader, I should have been strong enough to stand up for him. I should have been strong enough to tell the dissenting band members that I didn't feel the same way. I justified it but I never truly came to grips with it.

My other low moment (and it doesn't get much lower than this) was when I fired someone by letter. This band member had been with us for multiple years. My reason for letting this person go was because he was seemingly not very interested in the gig. He was subbing out a lot of the gigs. When he was on the gigs, it seemed like it was the last place he wanted to be. At the time, we weren't communicating very well. Because of these issues, and since it seemed like he wasn't that thrilled to be in the band in the first place, it seemed like it was time to let him go. He found out he wasn't in the band from a letter. Not a

Who's responsible?

phone call or a face-to-face, but a letter. As I sent the letter, I was under the impression it would be met with acceptance since I perceived his interest in the band was so slight and he wasn't on the gig very often anymore anyway. Well, I couldn't have been more wrong.

It was a huge mistake and one that I think of nearly every day. He didn't deserve to be treated like that. I failed him as a band leader and as a friend. It was cowardly on my part. To this day, we haven't spoken. Not because I'm upset with him but because after how I disrespected him, his reply to me was crystal clear. He has no desire to work with me or see me. Even if he wasn't interested in the band, that didn't mean he deserved my shortsighted and weak response to him, especially in written form. It's nothing to be proud of. Another lesson learned at the expense of someone else. Band leaders have that luxury to make mistakes at the expense of others who depend on you for a weekly paycheck.

The choices you make as a band leader are critical to the success of your band. How you go about it defines you within your band and to the music community you work with. Minneapolis and St. Paul, while great cities, are, at their core, small towns. Everybody knows somebody who knows somebody. When you make a mistake, people find out about it. If you're difficult to deal with as a leader, everybody finds out. If you're a leader who treats his band members with respect, everybody knows about that too. The goal for anybody working in this business is for longevity. Most musicians experience a time in their careers where they experience being hot and cold. Bands break up. Musicians switch bands. Changes happen in a business based on creativity. One thing that doesn't change is that each project needs a leader. For band leaders, the pillars of being a leader who musicians will want to work for are based on the basic things: get gigs, pay what you say you're going to pay, make great music, and get more gigs. Each leader will decide how they want to deal with the deeper darker secrets of their band members and business matters. However a leader decides to do it, it must be guided by respect and an understanding that people are depending on your wisdom, vision, and honesty to keep things going. If you falter at any moment, you stand the chance of being a leader of no one.

Taken on a windy, hot day at the Fargo Blues Fest in 2004. I remember we had a gig up there at 2:00 P.M., and then we had a gig at the Minnesota Music Cafe in St. Paul at 9:00 P.M. That's what we call, in the business, horrendous routing. It was a long day but, as usual, we got through it.

The highs and lows of perfection

Although *I've listened to music all my life,* I'd never call myself an expert or a historian about music. There are millions of hours of music I've never heard and will never hear. I've never been a music critic and had the luxury of getting thousands of records sent to me for my critique. I have nothing valid to say about classical, jazz, bluegrass, or any type of ethnic music. I simply don't own enough of those styles of music. As someone who loves music, I know I should but I know in my gut I'll probably never take the leap to educate myself.

Although I don't think I've reached the status of a musical curmudgeon, I show strong indications of being in a musical rut. I like what I like and it's hard to convince me otherwise. When I was a teenager and in my early twenties, if I read a review about a record and they said it was good, I'd go out and buy it. I owed that luxury to the lack of rent and car payments back then. I loved going to record stores and experimenting with new records. Most of the time, when I did that, it paid off quite well. As I grow older, the opportunity to just sit and solely listen to music is rare. Listening to the radio, your car stereo, XM, or Sirius Radio just isn't the same. Actually, I prefer the bumper music on talk radio stations more than the traditional local radio stations. At least you hear some variety. When I was a teenager, the solitary time with my Springsteen, Elton, The Clash, Elvis Costello, Bob Marley, Toots and the Maytals, Joan Armatrading, Graham Parker, and Van Morrison records, along with hundreds of others, was precious. I knew it had to be because it gave me so much pleasure. They helped define me as a teenager and young man. Those records molded my singing voice into what it is today.

One of the great things about records was arranging and displaying your records to your friends and strangers who came into your house. Take, for instance, the film *High Fidelity*. I like the scene in the film where John Cusack speaks to the camera from his living room, which could easily double as a record store. He talks about arranging his albums in various ways: musical styles, what record sparked a particular emotion in him, alphabetically, etc. That was so dead on. I did the same thing. It comforted me and gave me the feeling I was doing something important for the cultural good of mankind. One of the great things about having a huge record collection was the ability to make a great mixed tape. The science of creating an effective mixed tape could be as simple as just recording one record in its entirety, or it could be far more complicated and psychological. For me, the mixed tape was my artistic statement about how cool I wanted people to perceive me. I wanted to blow them away with the diversity of my musical collection and my knowledge. I used the mixed tape to try and get the attention of girls in public places. I used it to influence my friends into finding out about music they hadn't heard before. I used it so I could hear it at parties and hopefully impress everyone attending. The entire process of the mixed tape was extremely important to me, probably too important come to think of it.

The music we grow up to defines the music you hear today. Nobody is brilliant enough to create something completely original anymore. Even the giants who created rock and roll and the majority of the popular music we hear today had their influences. The established artists of today had to take their influences and dig deep to create their own sound. Thank God they did. That practice happens every day.

Perfection is another one of those words that's thrown about too casually, like genius or artist, or the phrase "oh my God" to the most mundane happening. When CDs came on the scene in the '80s, the claim was that it was as close to audio perfection as it could get. One of my favorite records, which happened to be one of the first digital recordings on an album, was Ry Cooder's *Bop 'til You Drop*. But I never really noticed too much of a difference until hearing my first recording on CD, Van Morrison's *Moondance* release. I heard it on a CD player that cost around $1,000 (remember how expensive small calculators used to be?). The sound was stunning. The songs jumped out at you. The acoustic guitar was so crisp and clean. Van's voice was stellar as usual, but more so. Everything was better. Everything seemed new. New things are like shiny toys. They gain your attention initially, but eventually the luster of the new thing fades. That's what happened with CDs for many people. The sense of touch played a very important role in my love of music. The touch of picking up a new record at the record store. I still remember how excited I was going to my local record store, Down in the Valley and picking up Elton John's *Captain Fantastic*. I had to have it. I obsessed about it. Seeing the fantastic cover and the back cover for the first time was exciting to me. Holding it in my hands and paying for it was exciting. Driving home with it anticipating the moment I put it on my turntable for the first time was a thrill. I loved reading all the great liner notes, the comic book, reading the history of the songs, etc. All of those things on all my records made an impression on me. Early versions of CDs didn't have all that stuff. It was the CD, the cover, the back cover, and that was pretty much it. Plus the cover was plastic. Getting the cellophane and tape off was a drag. It was structurally economical and it sounded great. The CD sounded perfect to me, but something was missing.

I missed seeing the record spin around when I listened to a CD. I missed the little noises all my albums made because, despite how much I loved them, I treated them very disrespectfully. Records would wind up out of the sleeves, against the walls, under my bed, stacked up on top of each other and worse. My records stood the test of my negligent abuse as long as they could, but everything has a limit. It didn't matter to me though. If I ruined the record, I'd just go out and buy a new copy. Any excuse to go down to the record store.

After hearing the CDs for a while, something still felt wrong to me. What I discovered was that I didn't want perfect. I wanted to hear the flaws. I wanted to hear the warmth. As much as I yearned for those things, I wasn't stubborn enough to ignore new technology. The availability of CDs was increasing and I wanted to pick up as many as I could afford. Perfection was within all of our reach with CDs. But the real source of perfection was the content within the CD.

Songs from my old records pop into my head all the time. I've often wondered what other musicians in the Twin Cities consider to be perfect musical moments. The moment in a song that always puts them in the place they were when they first heard it. Of course, there is no defining moment of perfection in anything, especially in music. There's always something that catches your ear that may replace one or modify your opinion of its perfection. All I know is that when I hear these pieces of perfection, it makes me smile and brings me back to a place that comforts and inspires me. In the immortal words of the universally accepted '80s shaman, Bobby Brown, as the author of this book I'm exercising "My Prerogative" and listing my Top Ten Perfect Music Moments. Following mine will be some favorite moments from others in the Twin Cities music scene.

Mick Sterling's Top Ten Perfect Musical Moments (not in any particular order):

1. The spoken intro, the guitar and bass groove on James Brown's "Sex Machine." Hell, who am I fooling? The whole damn song is perfect.
2. The guitar solo on "Candy's Room" from Springsteen's *Darkness on the Edge of Town* album.
3. The female background vocals singing "Once in a while, he won't call" on Van Morrison's version of "Its All in the Game" from the *Live in Belfast* album.
4. Tom Wait's version of *West Side Story*'s song "Somewhere."
5. The lines "For what are we / without hope in our hearts / that someday we'll drink from God's blessed water / and eat the fruit from the vine / I know love and fortune will be mine / somewhere across the border" from the song "Across the Border" from Springsteen's *Ghost of Tom Joad* CD. Also this line sung by Springsteen and Bobby King on his MTV *Plugged* CD: "Though the world is filled / with the grace and beauty of God's hand / I wish I were blind / when I see you with your man." Both of these lines make me cry like a damn baby sometimes.
6. Elton John's concert at Northrup Auditorium in the mid '80s when it was Elton and percussionist Ray Cooper.
7. The Hammond Organ solo and background vocals on the song "Are You Ready" from Bob Dylan's *Saved* album.
8. The background vocals of Little Steven Van Zandt on

the Southside Johnny and the Asbury Jukes record *Hearts of Stone,* specifically the song "Got to Find a Better Way Home."

9. When the band kicks in on Elton John's version of "Honky Tonk Woman" on his *11-17-70* album, specifically when someone in the crowd screams before he sings.

10. Ray Charles' seemingly drug-induced tempo and his vocals on "Drown in My Own Tears" from his *Ray Charles Live* record.

OK, one more: Joe Strummers' scream in the song "The Right Profile" when he says "It's Montgomery Clift Honey!" And the garbled pill-induced wailing of Montgomery Clift when he's pleading his case at the end of the song. I can't spell what he screams, so just buy the record and listen for yourself.

From Twin Cites-based songwriter Kevin Bowe:
(He asked me to mention that his perfect musical moments are completely random. His list of highlights is thousands long and changes every day. Here's what it was when I asked him):

1. Bob Stinson's guitar solo on replacements "Takin' a Ride" from their *Sorry Ma, Forgot to Take out the Trash* debut album.

2. Miles Davis' first note on the album *In a Silent Way.*

3. The sound of Bob Dylan's voice on the album *Bringing It All Back Home.*

4. Muddy Waters talking between songs on *Hard Again.*

5. Mick Jagger's vocals and everything on "I Don't Wanna Talk about Jesus" off *Exile on Main Street.*

From Minneapolis drummer and founder of the TC Jammers Bobby Vandell:

1. Listening to "Too Much" by Elvis Presley in 1956. I was three years old, I listened to it until the dog on the RCA label got dizzy. The way that record felt probably set the course for my life.

2. (A tie) Listening to The Underbeats at The Young America Center at the State Fair and hearing the drummer in The Velvet Hammers hit the bell of his ride cymbal.

3. Seeing and hearing Led Zepplin at the Guthrie Theater. The Guthrie is a small, intimate venue created so the human voice can not only be heard but also comprehended at a whisper in the back rows, with no amplification. You could feel John Bonham's huge twenty-eight-inch kick drum off the stage. Although it was miked, it seemed unnecessary. Jimmy Page's Marshall stack sounded simply perfect. I'll bet it was one of the only times he didn't have it on ten. I remember my jaw dropping and feeling scared, like some authoritative figures would arrive at any moment and shut it down and make it go away. It seemed wrong and illegal, like it was too good to last. I remember feeling like nothing in life would ever sound or feel quite like this, and nothing has yet. I'll never forget it.

4. The way Tower of Power's "Squib Cakes" breaks down in the middle and the drums (David Garribaldi), guitar (Bruce Conte), and organ (Chester Thompson) take over. That is the funkiest shit I've ever heard in my life. Just when you think you can't take it any more, the horns come back in. Every time I listen to that and the horns come in, I get chills.

5. Seeing and hearing Cannonball Aderly and Wes Montgomery when I was sixteen. Josef Zawinul, the great keyboardist who would ultimately start one of the most cutting edge, influential groups of all time, Weather Report, was in Cannonball's group at the time. They performed a song written by Zawinul, which was a hit for Cannonball at the time, called "Mercy Mercy." My mom brought me. I think she wanted to remind me of what true artists sounded like. I never have heard a guitar player as musical or one that sounded as beautiful as Wes Montgomery since. Cannonball, Wes, and my mom all passed away shortly after that. That concert was a gift from my mom that would last the rest of my life.

6. Seeing The Buddy Rich Big Band. They didn't need any amps. There is nothing quite as powerful as listening to a big band of that magnitude from ten feet away. If that doesn't move you, you're dead.

From Minneapolis singer and songwriter Mark Lickteig:
One for sure was when I was a kid, oh maybe five or six, I remember sitting with all my little cousins and listening to my Grandpa Lickteig on violin, piano, or organ, my dad on sax, my Uncle Ed on flat top guitar, my Aunt Teresa on piano—that's right two piano players playing the same old piano, one on the top notes one on the bottom half—my Uncle Albert singing bass so loud you couldn't hear anyone else, my Aunt Marg singing so high it hurt your ears, and my Uncles Bob and Tom singing the melody at Christmas or Thanksgiving gatherings. It truly was an example of how music was handed down through the ages. The way families used to entertain themselves—there was no TV, and the radio was only on for listening to the news

or baseball. That's when I decided if music makes people feel so good than that's what I wanted to learn to do. I can remember telling my mom after one of those "concerts" sitting in our "music" room in front of the radio speaker saying I wanted to be a music man when I grew up!

From Adam Levy of The Honeydogs:

1. Roberta Flack's "Do What You Gotta Do" from her 1971 *Second Chapter* LP. One of the most perfect intersections of song, vocal performance, production, and arrangement. Awesome band and orchestra—sounds live and played by all with great sensitivity. Tear jerking, soaring Roberta Flack vocal about letting someone go. Sad but hauntingly beautiful. I want this song played at my funeral.
2. One of my favorite songs is in Portuguese, "Baby" by Os Mutantes, a psychedelic Brazilian band from the late 1960s Tropicalia movement. Bossa Nova and the Beatles collide. Recently redone by Bebel Gilberto, I finally know what the lyrics are about: nonsense. Huge orchestrations. The cover is nice but the original is sexy as hell.
3. Barber's *Adagio for Strings*. Wow. Flat out beautiful after nearly one hundred years. The song builds and builds.
4. "I Want to Destroy You" by the Soft Boys. I'm generally a peaceful guy but anger, hate, and violence have never sounded so good. Simple guitar assault.
5. "Don't you Worry 'Bout a Thing" off *Innervisions* (1973) by Stevie Wonder. Absolute joy. Sounds like he had gobs of fun recording this little Cuban-inspired gem. Dizzying chord movement. Swinging percussion. A dozen acrobatic Stevies singing and playing at once. Transcendental.

From Blind Pig recording artist Renee Austin:

1. Singing the first song I ever wrote "When I Pray" in church one Sunday when I was fifteen years old. Scared stiff, I played piano and sang. It's still one of Mom's favorites.

2. I got nominated for a WC Handy Award for Best New Artist Debut. In one weekend I sang at the awards show and then filmed "Blues Divas" an upcoming eight-part public TV series by filmmaker Robert Mugge enlisting such incredible blues-women as Bettye Lavette, Odetta, Irma Thomas, Ann Peebles, Mavis Staples, Deborah Coleman, Denise La Salle, and myself. Filmed in the heartland of the blues in Clarksdale, Mississippi, at actor Morgan Freeman's Ground Zero Nightclub, the two-hour-long films present recent concert footage (shot during one long weekend) and intimate interviews conducted by Freeman, a Clarksdale resident and fellow blues buff. Morgan's also a good dancer and quite the ladies man.... He got up during my show and strutted his stuff. This weekend is definitely a magical moment.

From former Suicide Commando, currently the founder of the Springboard for the Arts in Minnesota, Chris Osgood:

1. Writing "Complicated Fun," a pop song I feel lucky to have written. I like it! And it was a song that wrote itself very quickly. For a fleeting moment I was able to have the creative experience that Plato described as being a "vessel of God." Yikes!

2. Seeing the Bonzo Dog Band at the Guthrie Theater (they opened for the Steve Miller Band) in 1969. They blew my ninth-grade mind!

3. Playing in Bo Diddley's band at First Avenue. Yow.

4. Teaching a particularly challenged guitar student at Knut-Koupée Music back in about 1982 how to tap his foot in time to music.
5. Every Richard Thompson show, most recently when he was at First Avenue in June 2004. At the time I thought the end of the club was imminent and when he went into "Wall of Death" it was such a metaphor for what that place was for me that I started to cry. I looked around and everyone else was crying too!

From Twin Cities drummer-percussionist Scott Sansby:

One of the all time greatest moments for me is about five minutes into Tower of Power's "Squib Cakes," during Chester Thompson's organ solo—when David Garibaldi goes to the bell of his ride cymbal, and his bass drum starts thumping a samba like pattern under Chester's B3 bass pedals and Rocco's funky walking bass line. Along with Bruce Conte's skanky rhythm guitar and Brent Byar's congas, Thompson's and Garibaldi's syncopations start weaving complex rhythms around the two and four that actually force my body to start squirming and twitching and dancing in place, no matter where I am or what I'm doing. My feet start tapping and my shoulders start shaking, and my concentration gets pulled from whatever I am doing at the time. It's almost as if a drug has just kicked in. This has been a constant occurrence for over thirty years. It works every time!

What makes this particular recurring moment especially powerful is the fact that I was in the right place at the right time, and my friend Tim McCarthy (then road manager for Kenny Logins) took me to see TOP at the Santa Monica Civic Center when they were taping a midnight special TV episode in 1973. At that show, they performed "Squib Cakes" before the record came out. Whenever I hear this song (which is at least weekly over the past thirty-plus years) I am transported back to that show and I can vividly picture the horn section leaving the stage and dancing through the aisles as the rhythm section tears it up on stage, grooving and vamping and laying down the funk in ways I had never seen it done before that night.

Another perfect musical moment that permanently altered my life was hearing Jimmy Smith's "Got My Mojo Working," for the first time in the mid 1960s. I think hearing this record for the first time was the moment that I was exposed to the intersection of jazz and R & B. The grooves laid down and the sound of the Hammond organ grabbed my soul and never let go. This is another record that I have been listening to at least weekly for more than four decades. To me there is still nothing more magical and intoxicating than that point about six minutes into this song when Jimmy starts to vamp vocally over his solo—talking about getting his roogalator working, and finally fading out singing "tootty fruitty oh rooty, oh rooty tooty fruity." To this day, I am still trying to find out what a roogalator is. Neither Mark Lickteig nor Paul Mayasich could supply the answer when the word came up recently.

The short-lived, one-tour and one-recording project, "Joe Cocker, Mad Dogs & Englishmen," represents an incredibly perfect moment in musical history. This 1970 tour and live recording—with an eleven-piece band, a ten-piece choir, and assorted friends and family members participating—remains an all-time classic. An incredible selection of songs, performed by an amazing group of musicians, and stamped with Joe Cocker's signature vocals is only made more perfect by the fact that this show was performed the two opening nights of First Avenue (then known as the Depot). While almost impossible to limit my choice to one selection from this album, I have to mention Leon Russell's and Bonnie Bramlett's "Please Give Peace a Chance." More of a groove, chant, and chorus than an actual song, this piece highlights the infectious, funky dance grooves this band—with three trap drummers and two percussionists—laid down under Leon's piano work, horn arrangements, and gospel-like choir . . . all focused by Joe's gravelly and soulful singing of a mere two sentences: "Give peace a chance, and the whole world will rock and roll. . . . Give peace a chance, and the whole world's gonna be a whole lot better." Timely and timeless. Perfect!

Every musician has his or her own list. What will surprise a lot of people is how diverse those perfect music moments are. More than likely, the perfect moments don't exactly coincide with the type of music you're used to hearing the artist play. The ones that seem to make it in this business have what musicians call "big ears." They're accepting of a lot of styles of music. It's the combination of all those styles that create the distinctive sound. As I get older, I don't take the time to appreciate my perfect music moments as much as I used to. Even though it's easier to have these moments with me at any time with iPods and car stereos, there's still plenty of time that passes between hearing these songs. I wish I could say that a lot of the new music will provide me an opportunity to add to my list, but I fear that won't be happening. It's rare that something moves me these days. Maybe I'm just getting too old and out of touch. I hope that isn't the case. My heart belongs to songs that moved me when I was younger. They inspired me. Everything I did musically partially came from those inspirational moments. It's always good to visit old friends every once in a while.

This was our huge stage outside of Bunkers for Heart & Soul in 2001. Notice the great shot of our friend, Luther Allison, on the Luther Allison Memorial Stage. The outdoor shows for Heart & Soul were filled with anxiety and craziness but, somehow, the show went on. From Little Feat, the Neville Brothers, and Jonny Lang, to Wayne Kramer of MC5, Indigenous, Susan Tedeschi, and Delbert McClinton, we had some moments on this stage.

I'm important dammit!

Chapter 12

During the political season of 2004, there was no shortage of musicians who'd become enlightened enough to share their wisdom with the nation. Film actors ranging from Leonardo DiCaprio, Ben Affleck, Cameron Diaz, and Ashton Kutcher, infomercial stars like supermodel Christie Brinkley, and music stars like Jon Bon Jovi, Little Steven, Dave Matthews, REM, John Mellencamp, and Bruce Springsteen, shared themselves with us. The script was the same. Everybody was saying basically the same thing, jumping on the same bandwagon. Elect anyone but Bush. It was a well-crafted and heavily promoted campaign. The Republicans had music stars like Lee Greenwood, Toby Keith, and Britney Spears, and TV and film actors like Ron Silver and Bruce Boxleitner. It's safe to say that in the celebrity endorsement campaign, the Republicans got their ass kicked, but despite that, they won this time. The Republicans definitely have some work to do on the caliber of their celebrity endorsement efforts for 2008.

All the celebrities just knew they were right and it was their duty to use their star power to tell you about it. As it turned out, despite the cavalcade of stars who sung and spoke their hearts out to encourage the young people to vote (vote Democrat preferably), the actual amount of young people who voted remained the same as in 2000. Lots of young people registered, but they didn't follow through with the actual process of voting. The fact that happened after such a gigantic push to get young people to vote had to sting a bit for all the celebrities involved. How do you explain it? You could blame it on television causing young people to have short attention spans, or maybe they just had something better to do on Election Day and couldn't be bothered. All of the star power fell short of the stated goal. As usual, the voice of our generation, Homer Simpson, summed up the celebrity worship world we live in when he uttered the words, "Rock stars, is there anything they don't know?"

We're drowning in mass media. The process of electing our president is featured on *Entertainment Tonight* in the same thirty minutes that also features opinions about the name of Gwyneth Paltrow's baby. They pursue rock stars and movie stars for their opinions on the political scene. I don't know if the media equates celebrity opinions in the same category as politicians or government employees. If they don't, you could never tell. Ashton Kutcher is considered in the same category of credibility as James Carville and Pat Buchanan for political savvy. The media seems to think we need to know how celebrities feel about political things. Me? Not so much.

I'm sure there may have been a time in popular culture when it was difficult for celebrities to express themselves politically. If they wanted to, they probably had to jump through some hoops and prove themselves knowledgeable about the issue before they were let on the air. In the '40s and '50s during World War II and the Korean War, Hollywood stars would express themselves by supporting the war effort and the troops wherever they were. If you didn't or expressed yourself negatively, you stood a good chance of being called a Communist, and that's no fun. It wasn't until the '60s and Vietnam that celebrities heard the call that it was time to share your feelings with the American public. From that moment on, having a celebrity share their opinion about a given topic is something we've grown to expect. You can either think it's fantastic or you can simply shrug and move on with your day. These days, I'm leaning toward the latter.

Every time I see a celebrity talk about politics I just keep experiencing a form of déjà vu. When the parade of celebrities and music stars grow, it feels like people are just playing a game of Follow the Leader. Maybe we never really escape junior high and high school no matter how hard we try. We all want to hang out with the cool people. If you go against the cool people, you run the risk of not being cool and being socially shunned. Sometimes in school you'd just get your ass kicked if you were different. As you grow older, that doesn't physically happen quite as often. The adult version of being shunned is being alone, being ignored sexually or an endless stream of misfortune that follows you at every turn. The musical version of shunning is that your fellow musicians mock you, or your work is immediately minimized because you're not being swept up in the passion of the current movement.

At the heart of it, the majority of celebrities and musicians want to be loved. They want to be accepted. They want to be deemed important. They want everyone to love what they do and nobody to hate it. Occasionally they take it to extremes.

At times, they want you to think what they think. If you don't think the way they think, you're ignorant or just plain wrong. Often times, this extreme type of thinking happens nationally and locally in all forms of the music business everyday. The music and celebrity world is just an older version of the cliques when we went to school. No matter what our outward bravado is telling you, deep down I think most musicians and celebrities hate to be criticized and hate to be viewed as just a musician or celebrity. As a local musician, I know I feel that way.

Musicians who speak out on political or social issues may feel more important, but when the cause or effort is complete they know they can always come back to what they know, being a musician. It's a luxury most citizens don't have. It's easier to put yourself on the line when you know you have something to fall back on. Musicians and celebrities have every right as citizens to say what they believe. The price you pay for putting yourself out there, being important, is the possibility of someone disagreeing with your viewpoint. That disagreement may affect your career.

There are two sides of the spectrum on this issue as with all issues. My yardstick is: Who actually gets things done? Who uses their celebrity to actually effect change? Who uses their celebrity to give exposure to the actual cause instead of themselves when they speak out? Here's my yardstick: Bono from U2 gets things done. Michael Moore wins awards and accolades, but doesn't accomplish much except to promote his own film. There's nothing wrong with promoting something you do, just don't disguise it as having expertise on such a broad subject. Michael Moore doesn't inspire. We need more people like Bono. They're hard to find, but we need to keep looking.

I remember reading an interview with Phil Collins when his career was red hot in the '80s. He had huge hits. He performed in Europe and America in one day for the benefit for the starving in Africa, Live Aid. He was asked during the interview if he concerns himself with criticism. His response was that if there are fifty thousand screaming people in the crowd and one person is not screaming or looks unhappy, he obsesses about that one person. As unrealistic as it would be, he would want to search for that person and ask them what they didn't like. That blew me away. Apparently no matter how successful you become, the same old insecurities always find a way to remind you you're not as important as you are perceived. I receive far more satisfaction than I should when receiving approval of my music, or from music that I like to listen to from outside sources. These are people who won't directly affect my career but I perceive their opinion as knowledgeable. They're around music a lot, so their opinion holds more weight with me. I'm talking about someone in particular, the man or woman who works at the record store.

I'm sure this yearning for their approval goes back to my first record store experiences at the little Down in the Valley location in Golden Valley when I was a teenager. I couldn't imagine having a better job than working at Down in the Valley. You could listen to new records all day. I thought everyone who worked there got free records all the time, free posters, shirts, and more. The most important thing was, if they liked a recording, it was probably something that I would or should like. Getting their approval, to this day, is still something that gives me pleasure. Granted, it's a little pathetic, but there it is.

One of my favorite films, *High Fidelity* with John Cusack and Jack Black, is a perfect example of the power of the record store employee. The clientele of their record store is mainly populated by young men desperately seeking the approval of Cusack and Black for everything they buy. They go out of their way to find new releases and obscure old releases and compare them with each other. Cusack and Black's characters know they're kings in this little court of theirs, each one dictating in their own way their dominance over the wannabes. The reality is, their opinion of their own lives is far less romantic then how the roomful of panting puppies they deal with every day perceive it. Reality can be skewed when your driving force is simply to impress someone you perceive as important.

Why do musicians care so much about the opinion of a single voice? A voice that in most cases has never created its own successful musical effort. Maybe it's about just wanting approval from someone we perceive as cutting edge or objective. Maybe we just crave the attention from a stranger. Why do we believe the great reviews and scoff at the bad ones? It could just be as simple as human nature to believe positive things about ourselves. However, what's worse is when nobody is talking about you.

The pursuit to be viewed as important is integral in most creative people. If you're a musician, you write, record, and perform. How you perform what you create is open to judgment. Most of the time it's strangers who are doing the judging. That can be tough sometimes.

I grew up reading reviews of artists in *Rolling Stone, Creem,* and other music magazines. I loved reading them. I also read Jon Bream's *Star Tribune* newspaper reviews of concerts that would come to the Twin Cities. Their opinion of an artist's performance or recording was important to me. When I was younger, it would play a role in whether I would purchase the record or go see the concert the next time the artist was in town. These days we're bombarded with options to see and hear music. When I was younger, hearing the music you loved would require you to lock yourself in your bedroom with a record or be lucky enough to be in the car for hours so you could hear your favorite song on the radio. The MTV-iPod generation could never understand what it was like before MTV. It was rare to see your favorite artists on TV. They weren't on *The Tonight Show.* No Letterman or Conan either. Listening to music wasn't something you had the opportunity to listen to eighteen waking hours of the day like it is now. Your favorite artists were somewhat sheltered from you for many hours a day. As far as seeing them perform, that was extremely rare. The main opportunity to see them was to go to their concert, which would only happen once a year, twice if you were lucky.

The only other source for an opinion about the artist came from reviews. I have nothing to back this up with; it's simply a hunch. My assumption is that the majority of reviewers are writers who are not musicians. If they had played an instrument, the majority may have wound up not being competent enough at their chosen instrument to become part of a successful recording or live act. Is it just another case of those who can do, those who can't teach? I don't think it's that simple. If it actually is that simple, it still doesn't explain the wealth of knowledge that reviewers have about music. You can take it to the next step and say that just because someone may know a lot about current music, is that person in the position to critique it, or should they be documenting it like a historian? To me, the evolution of the reviewer is just logical. If you love music but discover you're not strong enough at an instrument or vocally to take you where you want to be, or you have no chance of playing anything but you just love music, writing about music is a good way to stay involved in something you love. Plus, you get free concert tickets, free product, backstage passes, musicians hang on your every word and/or suck up to you nearly all the time. Not a bad gig if you can get it.

We perceive reviewers to have excellent taste in music. So excellent in fact that we let it play a role in our decision to purchase or go see an artist. Why do we do that? There are no diplomas a reviewer can hang on a wall like a doctor that declares their excellent taste in music. They've never met you before, so how could they know the listener will respond to any artist you hear? Some of the reviewers are too old to truly understand and appreciate the music they're reviewing. Since

I'm important dammit!

reviewers hear so much music, it seems logical that they stand a good chance of being burned out. Does that mean that a strong release might have received a favorable response from someone with fresh ears as opposed to a bad review from someone who's burned out? A reviewer of music wields a lot of power, ranging from the largest daily in the city or a suburban paper to an Internet expert who still lives in his or her mother's basement. His or her opinion can sway someone into buying or not buying the artist's CD. Their opinion can sway the way someone comments to their friends about a new effort from that artist. It's a lot of power. So much power, that most musicians respect it so much that they do everything they can to confront it, agree with it, disavow it, and run from it with equal passion.

To understand the component and the power of a reviewer, you have to put yourself in the place of a musician or songwriter. What if you were a bank teller? You had someone either visit your window or watch you from a video screen in another part of the building. What if that reviewer then wrote an article that hundreds of thousands of people would read? The reviewer's comments were that you'd "lost your passion" for your job, you "took too long to get to your deposit" or to "count your money that you want them to hand you," "the transactions you're doing today aren't nearly as good as the ones you did before," or "the transactions you're doing now are so similar to every other teller's transactions that you've now become irrelevant as a teller, soon to be a has been." That's what musicians can go through when someone decides to review what they do. The difference with a bank teller is that as long as you don't make a mistake or steal from the bank, you can most likely keep your job. If you're a musician, you stand a real chance of one person's opinion dictating the amount of money you will make and you may lose your job, or just want to give it all up. You can complain about it, or you can just be grateful someone's just writing about you.

One common complaint from local musicians is how entertainment and music writers decide who and what to write about. I know this because, for years, I was one of those voices. When I started to complain about it years ago, it was mainly me whining and feeling sorry for myself. The longer I perform, I still whine a bit, but I don't feel sorry for myself. Music reviewers and writers must focus on things that are new and bold, not as established and predictable as someone like me who's been playing in the Twin Cities for nearly twenty years. I get that, but that doesn't completely excuse them.

It's impossible to think that a reviewer or writer will pursue everything out there on their own. They rely on press releases from artists, record companies, management companies, and buzz from other writers and magazines for much about what they write. While it's true that some spend many hours in smoky bars or concert halls doing their job, what brought them to the club or concert venue is what puzzles most local players. What is it about the particular act they're writing about or reviewing that fascinated them enough to take the time to cover them in the first place? It could be as simple, such as the act is already established and the act has a strong promotional machine behind it to pester the writer into writing about the act. However, most local acts don't have it together promotionally. They depend on word of mouth and expect the writer to miraculously just hear about them and be so fascinated with the buzz that they'll show up to review or write about you. I wish it worked like that. I wished it for years. But it really doesn't.

Every year I'm involved with producing the Heart & Soul concert event in Minneapolis, I encourage artists to submit material to play at the festival. While it's important that I find established artists for name recognition purposes, having up-and-coming talent gives the event the depth I'm looking for. If the audience can discover newer talent at Heart & Soul, it just lends credibility to the event for the following years. In order for newer talent to get involved in any festival or perform at a club, they have to send some promotional material. The bands want to tell you about themselves. What the bands need to understand is that buyers want to know something about you, not everything about you. Brevity is beautiful. It gets to the point. Musicians need to get to the point in their bio packs.

When I read through band bio packages and listen to their CDs, here's what I want to see:

- A band photo, or individual member's photos,
- A one-page description of what the band does,
- A CD-Rom of a live performance (if possible, not necessary though),
- A song list if it's a cover band. If it's an original band, a song list from them doesn't mean anything to me because I've never heard them in the first place,
- Contact person and a business card with phone number, e-mail, fax number etc,
- A CD of no more than three songs, or a series of sixty- to ninety-second snippets in compilation form,
- I want the songs to move me. If they move me, I want the act,
- A Web site that's easy to navigate.

That's all I need to see. Here's what I don't want to see or hear:

- A package with no photo,
- A cassette with handwritten credits,
- A full history of each band members' music education. I don't care if they went to the Berklee College of Music. I certainly respect it, but in the end it really doesn't matter,
- A sheet explaining why the CD or cassette isn't quite done yet, but I'm supposed to look past that,
- Hearing a CD that is obviously so far out of the scope of what the club or festival normally presents. The artist wastes his or her money and product sending it and the buyer wastes his or her time opening the mail and listening to it in the first place. Before artists send material, they should learn about the venue they're sending it to.
- Understand where you're at musically. If you know you have work to do to get to the level of the artists playing at the venue or festival you're trying to get into, don't send your stuff yet. Wait a while until you're ready.

Another way for musicians to promote themselves is to send out press releases. The press release is one of the key ingredients for writers to notice you. The trick about the press release is that you have to craft it in the way that writers expect. Remember, writers receive press releases from labels from around the world every day. These releases are written by professional writers. Their main goal is for the artist they're working for to get noticed. The local musicians need to equate their own releases with what the pros send out.

Here are some tips for writing a professional press release:

- Make it one page, not five pages,
- Make sure you get to the who, what, where, when, and how in the first paragraph,
- Make sure the headline you choose tells the story and it will captivate who's reading it,
- Make sure you have your contact info on the top left of the page and at the bottom of the page,
- Make sure you're sending it to the right person,
- If you have someone doing this for you, make sure they're representing you correctly,
- Don't follow up your press release one hour after you send it. Give it a few days before you check back,
- Make sure you're available if your number is on it. If your agent or manager's number is on it, make sure they will be at the number listed,
- If the writer e-mails or calls you, you have to respond. Don't make them wait if they're trying to reach you. They won't wait long to move on to someone else.

It's really very simple, common-sense stuff to get your band publicity, but it has to be done right. Remember, the people who are finding out about you via a press release or bio pack are more than likely swamped with many other artists.

Unfortunately, in some situations the person who's finding out about you or claiming to support you doesn't have a lot of credibility to be doing his or her job in the first place. Or at least, that you may think.

What will never change in the music business is that there will always be some people deciding your fate that you'll find unqualified. It's the combination of cocky bravado and common sense that leads most musicians to that conclusion. It will always be frustrating that someone who decides your fate, either financially or artistically, is doing it from the position of never living in your shoes.

This goes beyond the stereotypical whining of a musician who didn't get his or her big record deal. People with little credibility and experience will occasionally decide the fate of musicians. That's a fact that we have to come to grips with and simply move ahead. People are choosing the music that we listen to today who lack the experience we would expect from someone in any other profession. It's always been like that, but these days, it's far more prevalent. In our everyday world, when we rely on someone's expertise we assume that the person giving us their opinion has had training and experience in what they are telling us. Most of the time we trust it. The music business isn't always like that. A musician's career can rise or fall by a gut feeling or someone listening to our stuff at an inopportune time. That's the risk we take working in a business that thrives on creativity and the artistic expression of music and the written word.

Every time I release a CD, I wonder if I should let reviewers hear it. My hesitation to send my work to reviewers is based on a few things. Will my CD just sit on someone's desk and never to be listened to? Will seeing my name on an envelope trigger an apathetic reaction from the reviewer? If they actually do listen to it, will their preconceptions of the type of artist I am cloud their opinion of it? If I do get review from someone, what is the true worth of it if it's just going to stay in the local market? All those reasons seem valid, but deep down I know it's not the main reason of my hesitation. At the heart of it, I just don't want to hear or read about someone not liking what I do. I want to be liked. I want to be viewed as a credible artist. I know that's a lot to ask from someone who just hears my CD, but it's still a fact.

I know that it's always good to have an objective set of ears hear my songs. I know I should be cavalier about it and say it doesn't really matter if a reviewer approves or disapproves of my effort. It's my artistic statement and I should stand behind it. I do stand behind my artistic statement, but that doesn't mean it doesn't hurt when someone thinks my artistic statement is garbage. Despite that, there is a light at the end of this self-doubting tunnel.

So who's really important? While you still have to deal with the decision makers in the business to get your work out there, the people who hear your music are the people who truly decide your fate. That's important. Reviewers and music writers will state their opinion about you and move on to another subject. In the end, reviewers are music fans and knowledgeable about what they're writing, but it's an opinion coming from someone eventually receiving a paycheck. It's unrealistic to think they can hear music the same way your fans or someone off the street hears your music. Their job is to be critical. The ones that do it well last in this business, just as other great bands and individual artists last when they do their job right. In the end, once you start writing reviews you've lost your ability to experience music solely as a fan. If you worked as a manager in a factory, you don't hang with the factory workers in the break room or at the bar at end of the shift. You're management now. You have to separate yourself and listen to music in a different head. That's the perspective music writers and reviewers come from. As a musician, you have to remember that when you receive criticism or praise.

Musicians have to remember that the most important opinions come from the people who have no other motive except to listen to your songs on a CD or in a live venue. If they like what you do and continue to support what you do, what more can you ask? Their support in the long run will do far more for you than the opinion of one reviewer or unqualified person in the music business. If the music you create moves someone, you've accomplished a lot. Providing a momentary soundtrack for people is a noble and worthy way to live your life. Settling for just that is nothing to be minimized.

I'm important dammit!

By far, the best picture of me as far as band photos go. I had a good hair night. Joshua Zuckerman took these photos a few minutes before were hitting the stage at Bunkers. My hair will never look like that again. My forehead is winning these days.

If ifs and buts were candies and nuts . . .

Chapter 13

There's an unwritten handbook in the music business. Considering how many times it's quoted, it may as well be the musician's version of the Bible. The lines quoted from this handbook are time tested. Once uttered, they achieve nothing tangible. They don't improve the situation, they don't change anybody's mind, and they don't get your money back. All these lines really do is provide musicians a way to vent. These lines are not nearly as effective stuck inside our brains for no one to hear. They must be spoken, loudly and forcefully, in order for us to achieve some type of resolution. This unwritten handbook comforts us in times of stress and when someone or something is unfair. It's not the kind of book you can tuck in your back pocket. This book has some girth to it.

The list of excuses, grievances, injustices, fan ignorance, and outright stupidity, jealousy, envy, incompetence, greed, poor timing, pettiness, and artistic-and-ego-driven gluttony are lengthy. For many musicians, recalling a particular topic from this list is the initial complaint route we take. Using this list can delay the eventual proof that whatever happened may not be someone else's fault. That's one of the reasons we use this book so often. It's never our fault.

My first real gig in a band was the first time I accessed this book. I didn't even know there was a book at the time. Not knowing about the book didn't stop me from accessing it.

My high school friends Mark and Tim Moran had a band called the T. Skeeter Band. It was an eight-piece band with horns, and I was the singer for the band. We would perform songs from Springsteen, the Blues Brothers, Chicago, Southside Johnny, and other rock and soul groups. One summer we found ourselves booked for a two-week stint at a resort up in Cross Lake, Minnesota, called Moonlight Bay. This gig was very important to our band. Our bass player (the namesake of the band) had just received a chunk of money from a relative. He decided to use some of this money to buy a new JBL sound-board and speakers for the band. At the time, we were playing on some Cerwin Vega speakers and monitors, which were very rough and didn't sound good at all. We basically used the system in Mark and Tim Moran's basement when we rehearsed, since we had no gigs to speak of. So the fact we would be playing on all new JBL gear was very exciting for us. It may have been exciting, but knowing how to make it sound good was another story.

As soon as the gear arrived, we jammed it in the Moran's basement and started wiring it up. Now when I say we, I mean that collectively, not me specifically. I'm an idiot when it comes to that. I still am. I'm not proud of it, but every man has his limitations. Eventually, the system was set up and ready to go. We turned it on, started playing, and let that JBL system blast. It was ear deafening and glorious.

Having this system was going to be a turning point for us. We were going to sound great up in Moonlight Bay. It was in the middle of the summer, lots of tourists. We were going to be living in the band house underneath the club. The potential for great gigs and available and willing vacation girls was big. We rehearsed a lot in the weeks before the gig. The night before our first gig, we took our caravan of cars and vans up to Cross Lake to start setting up to do our two-week gig.

Moonlight Bay was an old club that featured a huge hardwood dance floor, big bar, the complimentary Grain Belt and Hamm's Beer signs, and lots of bar stools. It was a slightly larger but stereotypical northern Minnesota bar. I know it sounds naïve, but we considered this gig to be important. It was our first real road trip; our first time we had played so many consecutive nights. We were eager to show the vacationers about our brand of Minneapolis music. We soon found out we didn't know what we were getting into.

Our first lesson was that our fantastic band house in Cross Lake was basically a dump. Not enough rooms, lots of wood paneling, old appliances, and other disappointments. Our lake access from our band house was a marsh-filled muck, so there were no late night parties on the dock after the gig, which meant no girls skinny-dipping after the gig. When you're in your early twenties, it doesn't really matter what a place looks like because our collective bedrooms or apartments we lived in were in far worse shape than what we were currently facing in Cross Lake. At this point, we were still optimistic about our gig. We were confident that we were the best band out there.

It was evident from our first gig at Moonlight Bay that our version of good was not the audience's version of good. It was clear that the volume coming off the stage was comfortable to us but ear-drum blasting for our audience. From the first couple of songs on the first night, every one of us in the band joined the long list of musicians before us to access the handbook.

The accusations we were leveling came fast and furious: "These people up here don't know what good music is, they're hicks, the owner was a fool, this house we're staying in sucks, the lake sucks, it was boring, it's not too loud because the lights on the board are still in the green, not the red." It went on and on. The bottom line was, they were wrong, and we were right.

As each night happened in the club, the response to us became even more lackluster and apathetic. We started dreading doing the gig. Our band house was getting to smell very funky and stuffy. That could be due to the fact that we jammed nine young men in their early twenties in a house that was built for four with one bathroom. It could also be due to the fact that one member of the band brought up a box of two hundred White Castle hamburgers that we kept in the refrigerator for far too long. The vision of cold, wilting Sliders is one that sends shivers down my spine to this day. Things were on a slippery slope. We were drowning our sorrows in stinky funk, not musical funk.

It was clear from the reaction of the crowd and the look on the faces of the bartenders and wait staff in the room that we just weren't working out. It's hard to be at a place where you're not wanted. What made it even more disappointing to me was the importance of the gig. I had visions of people loving our band, people asking for encores, validation of what we were doing. It didn't happen like that. With one night left on our two-week stint, the club called me into the office and fired us. It was a relief and a drag at the same time.

On the ride home, I kept going over all the things that went wrong. The resolution to all my introspection was that everybody was wrong and I was right. It couldn't have possibly been that we weren't that good at the time, or my voice wasn't nearly what I thought it was, or we didn't plan our song list very well to fit the room. I guess that's the beauty of being brash and young. You haven't learned yet how to give people the benefit of the doubt. And why would you when you're always right?

The easy accessibility of the musician's handbook is one of the things that minimize musicians. My introduction to this handbook pales in comparison to how other bands were introduced to it. I'm just a suburban kid from Crystal, Minnesota, who liked to sing and found himself in a band. But even my little northern Minnesota escapade has the opportunity to shed some light about the local scene in general.

I heard a great phrase in 2004 that summed this all up: If ifs and buts were candies and nuts, every day would be Christmas Day. When something good happens, the chances are greater that it happened because of something you did to make it happen. It most likely didn't happen because you were lucky. When unfortunate things happen, the chances are greater that it happened because of something you did to make it happen, not bad luck. Instantly blaming your misfortune on bad luck or unfair and unethical people (while those are to blame occasionally) is too easy an out. Making hasty judgments hinder our careers. This is hard pill to swallow for musicians, or anybody for that matter. Not taking responsibility for the status of your career is like a band-aid that keeps falling off the wound. The excuses cover the wound for a while but somehow that wound keeps finding a way to expose itself.

My career in the Twin Cities has been filled with compromises and excuses. Any musician has both of those tools in his or her arsenal. I'm a driven person who likes to accomplish a lot of things. I've accomplished more than a lot of local musicians. But the fact that for the past sixteen years the financial level of my chosen profession of being a professional performer has remained at relatively the same level.

I still get paid the same amount per gig at clubs as when I started playing. I'm still playing in clubs. I still worry about where my next gig is coming after the busy summer season. Even though I have a name in town that a lot of people recognize, being recognized doesn't translate to putting butts in the seats. There are a thousand reasons I could site as to why this is happening. At times, I say those reasons out loud. But in my gut, I understand the reason my career is where it is.

Fear and insecurity are within all of us. With musicians, occasionally those traits can instigate brilliant creativity. In others, those traits keep you down. For me, it inspired me to maintain the level of keeping my head above water.

Being able to maintain is an accomplishment that I'm proud of. A lot of musicians aren't able to rise up to the level of maintaining. Maintaining your standard of living is something that anybody responsible for a family strives to do. Throughout my effort to maintain, I've had some great moments I'm very proud of, but in the end, from when I wake up in the morning to when my head hits the pillow after I get home from a gig, all my efforts are focused on maintaining. I've been fortunate enough to carve out a respectable reputation in town. I get work. I get summer outdoor festivals. I get private gigs. The combination of all those types of gigs provides my band members with a steady weekly paycheck. Sometimes the number on the check is healthy and sometimes it's paltry. Fortunately, the guys I play with have a lot of their own things going on, so the urge to explore, tour, or take big risks is not as strong as in other bands. The talent level of the people I play with could easily place them in a higher level of their profession. Each one of them is a grown man. Their professional status at this point is something they have to deal with every day. I'm grateful that they've decided to work with me. I'm a better performer because of it.

I'm a hard worker. I love my job despite not being in the position I thought I'd be twenty years ago. Occasionally, people come up to me when I perform and ask me why I'm still playing in clubs. My standard answer is, "I don't know, it's a weird business." My real answer is one they really don't want to hear in a bar conversation.

I realize that what I do is special. I can sing. I'm better than a lot of singers, but there are plenty better than me. I'm a strong front man. I can write strong songs. I can inspire people. I can make a difference. I can use my profession to help others. I'm a good papa to my kids and a good husband to my wife. I've been a good son to my mother and a good brother to my sisters. Those are things I can take credit for.

On the other hand, on occasion, excuses and compromises have altered my professional career. At times, I've refused to accept lessons that were staring me in the face. I've let jealousy and pettiness cloud my judgment. I've been envious of musicians who are farther along than I am. I've avoided risks I could have taken. I've settled for situations just to avoid a confrontation instead of banging heads with that person to get my way. As uncomfortable as those issues are to deal with, I have to own up to these traits as much as I own up to my positive traits.

All those reasons are why I'm where I'm at today. Even though there are times when self-pity creeps in, I see what's out there. I'm happy I'm where I'm at. If things improve, fantastic. If things stay the same, I'm still making music and getting paid for it. For better or for worse, that still works for me.

These three photos were taken on ranch property in Grand Coulee, Washington.
Every summer, Kristi and I would take Tucker and Mikalea to the birthplace of
Kristi and her mom. It's burning hot in the summer. The locals always think we're
crazy because we get dressed up and take cool photos. You can tell by these photos
about the unique nature of my kids. Just look at those faces. Tucker and Mikalea
used to stop traffic when they walked into a room. They still do these days.

Who's your daddy?

Chapter 14

I **never carry pictures of my kids.** I really should but I never do. I know myself too well. I'd lose them, or the pictures would be bent beyond recognition. I'd be doing a disservice to my kids by the way I'd treat those pictures. Even when they were babies, I never carried pictures of them. My wife, her parents, and my parents had spectacular shots of the kids that we hung in our house and displayed in photo albums. When they were babies up to around four years old, we took a ton of video footage of the kids. These videos really captured the unique nature, humor, and kindness my kids possessed. Although my kids always looked amazing in photos, I always figured the best way to see my kids was to meet them.

From the moment they were born, it was clear to me that my kids were the greatest thing I'd ever be involved with. Being a parent defined me as a man. As a working musician who was married with two kids, it presented certain circumstances (not challenges, but circumstances— there's a big difference) that also defined me in a deeper sense. As soon as my first child, Mikaela, appeared in the delivery room, I became a grown-up. When my son, Tucker, was born, I grew up even more. I became someone who was here to protect them. What I also realized was that I was not going to be the kind of parent who did what was expected. As a father who was choosing to make his career in music, the concept of normalcy was thrown out the window. I was a father and it was time to go to work.

Preconceived notions are annoying. Since no one can predict what will happen from one moment to the next, the amount of credence we give our preconceived notions is surprising. When any young couple finds out they're going to have a baby, it seems everyone has an opinion that simply must be heard. When people hear musicians are involved with an upcoming birth, the opinions and suspicions you can hear from people are plentiful and mostly unwelcome. The natural assumption is that a musician's child will experience more ups, downs, and uncertainties than being a child of someone who has an established and safer job. My experience tells me that those preconceptions couldn't be farther from the truth.

When my wife told me we were having a baby, my first reaction was to laugh hysterically. While it was a natural extension of our marriage and our history since junior high school, the concept of me being a father amused me. Strangely, I wasn't afraid or freaked out about it. That may be due to my years of taking care of my sister, Jessica, when she was a baby or just my affinity with kids in general. I had a feeling of liberation during a time when it would be easy to feel like a piece of your personal freedom was slipping away. My world opened up when we found out that we were having a baby. My brain started spinning with ideas.

When people first hear the news about your pregnancy, everyone is thrilled. As the birth gets closer, people start dropping hints about what it will be like when the baby arrives. As the event comes even closer, people start becoming soothsayers and start telling you what the first few days of the baby will be like. When you're in the ninth month, they start saying things to your wife or girlfriend about how uncomfortable they must be and when is that baby coming out? Another interesting thing that happens when your wife or girlfriend is pregnant is that people naturally assume they can touch and rub her belly at will, simply because a pregnant woman caught their eye. The baby inside my wife became community property until the baby came out. That part of my wife's pregnancy drove me crazy. I never touched another woman's breast because they were wearing a blouse that caught my eye. It's a curious little world we live in at times.

As with any first-time parents, we had the universal concerns. Could we handle this? Would we be good parents? Will the baby be healthy with all ten fingers and toes? Stuff like that. During this time, I was playing in a band that was rarely playing in clubs but was taking up a huge amount of my time driving back and forth between rehearsals. At the time, I was a waiter sporting a super sexy flowered shirt and khaki shorts at place called The Good Earth. I was walking out with a whopping $20 in my pocket for each lunch shift and $40 for a dinner shift, if I was lucky. It was clear from the money I was bringing in that my kid wasn't going to be getting a pony any time soon. My wife was doing her own jobs as well, thankfully making more money than I. We were surviving, but we were both concerned about finances with a new baby on the way.

I assume most club musicians face the same issues when they start a family. Creativity and artistic drive can overwhelm the need to be practical. It can prohibit you from going out and finding a more secure job with benefits and insurance. The perception some musicians may have is that those kinds of jobs are for other people who aren't dictated by creativity. The only problem is, when that baby arrives that baby couldn't care less what job you have, as long as you do your job as a parent and make them laugh while you do it. You've got to find a balance between your artistic and practical side if the money just isn't coming in from your music.

One remarkably sad aspect of the music scene in any city is how little money local players actually make. The Twin Cities is actually one of the places where the money being made is somewhat acceptable. When I say acceptable, I mean that the bands normally don't walk out with $10 in their pocket after a gig and/or they don't have to pay the club to play there. I've been playing in Twin Cities clubs for more than twenty years. During those years, and prior to that, it seems that the magic figure to reach for is $100 per band member. That's what the clubs have been holding out as the standard. That's the standard most local musicians hold as the goal to meet, which will dictate whether they take the gig or not. This figure has not been adjusted for inflation or the cost of living in general in the other aspects of your life like every other product that has ever existed. In a larger sense, that particular issue is something that local players will have to address eventually. One hundred dollars per member can't suffice forever. Either the musicians need to demand more from the clubs, or the clubs need to start charging more at the door for the bands.

Musicians and clubs are constantly at risk financially. Demanding more money from a club so you individually make more money is a risky proposition. If you ask for it, you better have the numbers to back it up. Your band can be more musically superior to other bands, but unless you put butts in the bar stools and booths, your plea for more money will be dismissed. Money is always at the forefront of a musician's life. A musician adding a new baby in his or her personal life adds an element of stress and concern. A musician depending on this level of income to support a new baby in his or her life, without any other source of income to supplement it, soon realizes he or she is in a predicament.

Another thing you realize during the time before the birth is that no matter how cool you think you are, you start to realize that there are some things you'll have to do in the upcoming months that are just not that cool, such as Lamaze classes, visits to the doctors, reading baby material, looking for baby stuff, going to baby showers, etc. All people want to talk about is the baby. The concept of talking about what you're doing musically or creatively starts taking a back seat to the thing that keeps kicking your wife or girlfriend and making her have to pee every hour on the hour. Bearing that in mind, it's vitally important that the cool factor is relayed to this child. Since the mother is doing all the hard stuff during the pregnancy, this is one thing the father can shine in (because as I found out, a man is useless in Lamaze classes), if they're interested.

I made a conscious decision right away that my baby would be the coolest. He or she would have to listen to the essential stuff in the womb. Van Morrison, Springsteen, Elton, Aretha, Otis, Pickett, Sam and Dave, Joan Armatrading, Elvis Costello, The Clash, James Brown, Southside Johnny and the Asbury Jukes, The Judds, Merle Haggard, Kristofferson, Johnny Cash— my baby was going to know all the words before he or she arrived. When my new baby daughter did pop out and didn't know the words, I didn't hold it against her. She was too busy peeing, pooping, eating, and sleeping for me to discuss it with her. I figured I'd wait a few years for her to catch up. Learning how to talk first would be a helpful tool I supposed.

Just because a child is in your life, doesn't mean the quest to advance your career in the music business diminishes. In some ways, it intensifies because now instead of working for yourself, you're now working for the future of your child. If you're a local player, the natural response is to find more club gigs and private gigs to bring in more money. You can also explore getting studio gigs for industrial or commercial work.

If you're a songwriter, trying to place your songs with artists who will record your songs is a method, but that takes a while to realize a result, if any result happens at all. Your creativity and artistic skills need to get the job done. If you're not working, that means no money is coming in. On the other hand, if you're not working, you have the opportunity to spend more time with your child.

Even though I came to terms with this a few years ago, I occasionally become envious of artists who are on the road and living the life. There is a certain romance to it. Even after knowing how much downtime there is between gigs, the thought of being on the road is intriguing. The attraction of playing in front of your fans and a whole new crowd of people discovering and accepting something you've put so much time into is very strong. You don't want to become too practical, though. As corny as this sounds, somewhere in your gut you have to hold on to the concept that at any performance, something may happen that could make you a star. I still have that. It just whispers to me from a place of relative contentment instead of literal desperation.

There could be many reasons why I didn't put my band on the road. The obvious one was that there were ten to twelve people who would have had to be on the road. That would have been tough to achieve any financial success playing in clubs. Other reasons can't be put on an expense sheet, but are still viable. I liked the comfort of knowing my audience and the clubs we were playing. While, at first glance, playing a club in another city is attractive, what you find out most of the time is that the club in the other city is just like the one in your hometown or many times worse. So now you find yourself in a strange city, making no money, you can't sleep in your own bed, and you're bored and lonely. It's another glamorous part of this business.

The biggest reason I didn't want to go on the road was that I didn't want to miss anything with my kids and my wife. I'm not one of those video camera carrying freaks who records absolutely everything my kids do. On the other hand, I realized how precious this time was. The way I viewed it, if I was on the road for thirty to ninety days at a time, that was one to three months of time of my children's life that I would never see. I would've lost the opportunity to laugh with them, read stories, dance with them, take them to the laundromat and push them around in the laundry cart, introduce them to the world of *The Simpsons,* take walks, ride bikes, watch the film *Dumbo* on video in the steamy bathroom to clear their lungs when they have the croup, mess around in the yard, make them breakfast in the morning, hang out at McDonalds, hold them when they are sad or crying, and a thousand other things. The tradeoff just wasn't worth it.

I'm not insinuating that I was destined to achieve huge national success. But what I am saying is that I was in a position when my kids were babies to put my band on the road similar to the hundreds of other bands that tour the blues club and summer blues festival circuit. The band was strong enough to do that. I was a strong enough front man to achieve a consistent level of success that would have provided the members of the band hundreds of dates per year around the country. While that would have been rewarding to my ego for people from around the country to praise my band and me, the alternative was staring me in the face. The fast food, empty hotel room, not sleeping in the same bed with my wife, not seeing my kids go to bed or waking them up in the morning, not to mention the financial risk of leaving our weekly gigs, made my decision to pursue my musical interests locally make sense. If I'd thought that the rest of the band had a burning desire to hit the road, I would have had to adjust my thinking or contemplate even being in the band. Fortunately for me, my band seemed content to stay in town and make money playing in my band and other side projects. I never really thought of it as giving up on the dream. I perceived it as just being realistic. There are many occasions where working musicians find themselves on the road. It doesn't really matter if the tour consists of clubs or stadiums. It doesn't matter if the hotels are five-star or Motel 6s. It doesn't matter if the band is depending on merchandise sales to survive or each band member clears $10,000 a week plus per diem. If you have a family and you're on the road, you separate yourself from your child. In every profession, occasionally you're going to find some deadbeat who's so selfish or deluded that ignoring his child or never seeing his child because it's an inconvenience to his career goals is justifiable. There are a percentage of musicians that are like that, but from my experience it's minuscule.

The benefits of being a child of a musician are many. For my kids, they got to do things that none of their friends could ever dream of doing. Going backstage at concerts, meeting other musicians, actually being on stage when Jonny Lang played at Heart & Soul all those years. Meeting former Governor Jesse Ventura at Heart & Soul. Meeting present Governor of California, Arnold Schwarzenegger, at Planet Hollywood for a Camp Heartland benefit. Going behind the scenes and actually becoming friends with the kids from Camp Heartland. There were many experiences that my kids were fortunate to experience, and they benefited from all of them.

Another bonus was the interaction that other musicians have with kids. In general, the way musicians interact with kids is more natural than people who work in other professions. They don't talk down to kids. They welcome the creativity of kids. They don't naturally assume that if they meet a kid who's got energy or acts a bit unusual, the kid needs some type of medication to calm them down. They like it when kids are still kids. That may be because, as musicians, we never lose the child in us and we identify with them more than others. I'm convinced that their interactions with other musicians and the situations they experienced with musicians gave my kids a broader and more objective view of their world. Plus, when their friends find out they have a papa who's a musician, even on the local level, they get treated differently. Their friends think it's cool, probably cooler than what their own parents do. And that's despite the fact that their parents probably live in a house worth far more than my house and they have newer cars. The concept of cool prevails over material things when it comes to perceptions of another parent.

I've been blessed to have a woman who loves me. I'm blessed to have a woman who understands and supports my career. She has always understood that it's part of my job to speak to people who see the band, and that includes women who may show interest in me. I'm blessed to have a woman who encouraged and welcomed the way I played, and cared for and taught our kids. Mostly, I'm blessed that my wife has shown such patience with a career that is financially precarious and totally dependent on the whim of music lovers. Having a partner who believes in what you do plays a huge role in how successful, content, and creative a musician can be. As someone who makes his living playing in bars, I fully realize that if I were a single father raising two kids things would be different. The wisdom and kindness that our kids received from my wife will live with them all their lives, and it will be relayed to their kids when they start a family. That's huge stuff. Doing well by your kids is the common man's legacy.

Unfortunately for all kids, the fact that my kids live in a two-parent household to this day puts them in the minority. This may be viewed as politically incorrect, but the fact that my kids have a man and a woman guiding them is huge. That's not to say that a single woman or man, or two men or two women, couldn't raise a great kid. If the choice is a child not being raised by caring people at all, of course it's optimal to have the child raised by whatever combination is available and agreeable to the child. But common sense tells me that the natural instincts that women have for kids differs from men. I'm not being sexist, it's just how I see it. Some things are just a fact. Those differences mold kids. It's unfortunate when a kid misses out on those perspectives from a man and a woman every day.

My wife would read books to my kids. They'd sit on her lap and look at pictures, make the noises the animals in the books make. She liked being quiet with them. She took them to bookstores and strolled around for hours. She took them to a Middle Eastern restaurant because that was one of her favorite foods to eat when she was pregnant. I made stories up and told them. I tickled them and threw them up in the air. I put them on my back or my neck. I jumped on the bed with them. I shared my weird sense of humor with them. The fact is, my wife naturally did things with our kids that I wouldn't have come up with myself. I did things with our kids that my wife would never have dreamed of doing. What made it work is that we both gave each other the respect to raise our children collectively, but also understanding that within our collective partnership there had to be some room for individual interpretations of a man and a woman. There's a saying that goes, "You don't know what you don't know." Kids who don't experience the unique interpretations of being raised by a man and a woman every day will view the world differently from a kid who was raised by a man and woman in love who guide their kids every day. It's the ideal scenario that I wish every child could experience. Fortunately for our kids, they did. Our kids' persona reflects my wife and myself. I couldn't imagine them being raised by either one of us individually. Could it have happened? I suppose, but they'd be different kids.

As someone who performs music locally, there are many times I'm conflicted. I enjoy my job. I love what I do. However, the career choice I made does not provide the financial stability that I would prefer for my wife and my kids. I'm envious when I see our kids' friends or my wife's friends with beautiful houses in the suburbs with two to three new cars. I don't have the financial resources or stability to take long vacations on a whim. We live in a modest house. I'm gone most nights. I spend a lot of time on things that either never have a financial return, or the financial return comes much later than when I performed the task. It's not easy living with someone who performs in clubs for a living. It's not a lifestyle that caters to someone who's insecure about his own self-worth or has a tendency to become jealous. It also requires that someone look past the material things they're missing by living with someone who depends on performing at the local level.

What being a performer has provided for my kids is the chance for them to be exposed to music since before they were born. They get to see me communicate with people. They get to see me make people happy. They get a chance to experience creative people in many aspects of the music business. They learn important things about respect, being prompt, delivering on your promises, hard work, kindness, humor, and many other things. Most importantly, my kids get to have fun. A lot of fun.

They didn't get everything their friends got. They weren't spoiled. We expected—and demanded—respect and they gave it to us. We respected them. My wife and I had a great time raising our kids from babies to teenagers. They blessed us. My profession is a blessing for my kids. Tucker and Mikacla are blessed to have such a wise and tenderhearted mama. Despite some financial shortcomings I may have because of my profession, I go to sleep every night knowing deep down in my gut that I'm a lucky man.

Bunkers. It all began there for me in this town. Before my Sunday nights, I was destined to flounder. Let's just say, without this club, life would be far more difficult for me. For me and hundreds of other musicians, they make us feel like we're home.

The long ride home

*O*ne nice thing about being a musician is that you avoid all traffic jams when you drive home from work. No construction, no road rage. Just overnight delivery trucks, graveyard shift workers getting to work, and potentially drunk drivers are the obstacles we have to deal with. I've been driving home from my job of singing in nightclubs for more than twenty years. It's with a mixture of relief, anticipation, and apprehension that greets me when I pull out of the club parking lot and start the long ride home. This is a period of time that can provide musicians with much needed perspective or fuel misconceptions. It can provide you time to come up with potentially new and hopefully great ideas for songs, or give you time to decompress. It can give you time to figure out the next steps of what you want to achieve with your career and your family. If you're around people all day, it's the one time you can truly be alone with your thoughts. If you're alone, it's more time alone as you go home with no one there. The main theme of all musicians' thoughts during this time is probably wondering why they continue to make this drive each night and hoping that someday they won't have to make it. The long ride home and how you respond to it plays a role in what you see when you see a musician on stage.

I've been a big believer that being a musician is really not that much different from any other job. The basic principles apply to all jobs. You've got to know how to do your job. You punch in, you punch out. You need to know how to work with different people. You need to know how to play the game in your workplace. You're always looking for a way to move ahead and, of course, make more money. While this next principle happens in the business world, it's magnified in the world of music. This principle being that if you're better at something, you should be more successful. We've all seen musicians and singers who make you wonder why they aren't more famous. Why are they still playing in clubs when they're so good? Why doesn't this band have a record on the charts? The questions you hear from fans are numerous and sometimes hard not to take personally.

Their intentions are good. They like you and they want you succeed. Maybe there's an element in play that they want to say they knew you once when you do succeed. However, it's a question that would never be asked of any other profession. That same person wouldn't ask a car mechanic while he is fixing their car to tell them why he's still fixing cars. They won't ask the mechanic why he isn't running the mechanic shop or why he isn't making his own engine or car. People don't expect that type of ambition and creativity from other professions. They expect it from musicians. I don't have a problem with that, it's just peculiar to me.

The ride home is also your opportunity to weigh your options. It's no surprise to anyone that musicians get propositioned for various things quite often. This can range from invitations to a house party after the club closes, to drugs, and most of the time, the potential of immediate sex or beginning the process that will eventually lead to sex with someone. How you handle those options keeps your mind buzzing for a while after the gig.

The stage can truly be your best friend and your biggest promoter. It can transform you into someone you would never imagine if left to your own devices. It forces people to pay attention to you. People listen to you. Most of the time, you're performing on a raised stage, which means you're not on the same level as others; people are literally looking up to you. Off stage, the musician may have many things that attract people to him or her, but there's no way they're as attractive as when they're on stage. The potential for many offers can happen every night you perform. The options musicians have are limited to three choices: either you accept the immediate satisfaction of what is being offered, you walk away from the offer, or you walk away from it and you ruminate on multiple long rides home about it. The "what ifs" and the "well, if I did this, I could make it happen" ideas are a key element in the long ride home. What makes the decisions easier or harder for the musician is usually what awaits them when they actually arrive home.

In a perfect scenario, home for musicians (for everyone for that matter) should be a place of safety, creativity, and contentment. When you drive home from a gig, you should arrive at a place that wraps your arms around you and welcomes you. Whether it's a huge house or a studio apartment, the concept of home is very powerful for some musicians. If what awaits you at home is daily conflict, aggression, and suspicion, how you weigh the options presented to you at the club that night may be different.

I'm confident that everyone experiences his or her own version of the long ride home. For most people, it happens in the late afternoon or early evening. I just can't imagine it reaches the magnitude of a musician when they drive home from a gig. Driving home at six in the evening with a highway full of traffic has too many distractions. It can't compare to the solitude of the two in the morning ride. The time of the night can serve as a great tool for musicians to focus on what's positive about what they're doing. Unfortunately, the essence of the creative urge is normally fueled by the realization that you're never satisfied with the status quo. You can either blame your status on how you perceive everyone is teamed against you, the ineptness of your band mates, your lousy agent, the lousy audience that night . . . the list can go on and on. Sometimes all it takes is a mistake on one particular song that night that sets you off. Maybe it's something that's happened before. Maybe you see it as a problem that is magnifying every time you perform the song. If you keep these feelings to yourself, it festers each night and you add it to the long list of things in your car on the long ride home. It's these insecurities that slow down or simply eliminate the opportunity presented to all musicians for their own time to create and improve their situation in their profession.

Although I've never been on a national or international tour, or been gone for months at a time on the road with a band, I've paid my dues on the road. For all of you who think it's glamorous and exciting, there's a certain level of truth in that. The more popular you get, the more well known you are, Your glamorous and exciting opportunities become more frequent. Most the time, though, every musician has his or her version of the long ride home. It may be in a $250,000 custom RV, a private plane, or in the back of a fifteen-seat GMC van with the whole band and all your gear shoved in it. The routine is still the same. The battle is the shadow of boredom and loneliness that always follows you when you're on the road. The actual performance is such a small piece of the day. What do you do with the other twenty hours? That's the tricky part for all musicians.

As creative beings, musicians should never be satisfied with where they're at professionally. That restlessness causes hasty decisions, and sometimes very wrong choices for our professional and personal lives. As audience members, what you see each night from your favorite player is the culmination of a series of decisions that were derived from childhood all the way through what they did the night before. The long ride home serves to focus all these things for musicians.

Sometimes an issue will only last one night. Sometimes they can last for months or years. To quote Neil Young, "Rust never sleeps." These tried and true issues will always be on the tip of the tongue for all players and haunt us on the long ride home. Why am I still playing this club? Why don't I have a record deal? Why hasn't my record sold more than that band's? Why is one band getting more work than my band even though my band clearly can kick their ass? I'm better than they are! What am I going to eat when I get home? I hope there's some cookies left. Cold pizza sounds good. The hits just keep on coming. I love this business.

OTHER BOOKS FROM CROTALUS PUBLISHING

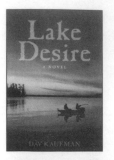

Lake Desire by Dāv Kaufman
Drama/Fiction, 240 pages, hardcover, 5.5" x 8.5"
ISBN 0-9741860-0-7

This touching novel chronicles the interconnected stories of twelve residents of the small fishing town of Desire, Minnesota, after a boating accident takes the life of Elle Ravenwood, the town's most loved resident. Bear, a biker and tattoo artist, has made it his religion to sit on the dock on the shores of Lake Desire every morning to write of the melancholy magic that swept over the town after Elle's death, and gives all of them the power to change their lives.

Roadsides: Images of the American Landscape by Kelly Povo
Photojournal/Nonfiction, 112 pages, hardcover, 10" x 8"
ISBN 0-9741860-3-1

Through images of diners and cafes, bowling alleys and bars, drive-ins and motels, photographer Kelly Povo has spent the past twenty years capturing the essence of these places on the road. Her photographs invite us to revel in their unique designs, and perhaps even find memories in these "slices of Americana" that dot the American landscape. Featuring informative, historical, and enlightening text by Bruce Johansen.

North: Stories and Photographs by Dāv Kaufman, Martin Springborg, Kelly Povo, Phyllis Root, Dr. Daniel Keyeler, Dr. Barney Oldfield, Terry Pepper, Bill Marchel, Jeff Richter
Nonfiction, 112 pages, hardcover, 11" x 8.5", ISBN 0-9741860-4-X

Through a selection of talented writers and photographers, the North is embodied in the stories and photographs of the pursuit of albino deer in the central woods of Wisconsin, of the lifelong search to encounter a moose in the wilds of northern Minnesota, of trailing timber rattlesnakes in the Mississippi River bluffs in southeastern Minnesota, and in many others. Each of the artist's chapters offers a dramatic perspective of the region we love—each of them welcoming us North.

Proof: Ruminations on the Everyday by Martin Springborg
112 pages, paperback, 11" x 8.5", ISBN 0-9741860-1-5

Proof: Ruminations on the Everyday is a photographic journal; one artist's effort to document everyday life in photographs. One photograph was made each day over the course of one year, the resultant collection of images glorifying the commonplace.

Order direct from www.crotaluspublishing.com or wherever books are sold.